INTRODUCING
NEUROPSYCHOLOGY

INTRODUCING NEUROPSYCHOLOGY

The Study of Brain and Mind

By

STUART J. DIMOND, Ph.D.

Reader in Psychology
University College
Cardiff, Wales

CHARLES C THOMAS • PUBLISHER

Springfield • Illinois • U.S.A.

Published and Distributed Throughout the World by

CHARLES C THOMAS • PUBLISHER

Bannerstone House

301-327 East Lawrence Avenue, Springfield, Illinois, U.S.A.

© *1978, by* CHARLES C THOMAS • PUBLISHER

ISBN 0-398-03794-9

Library of Congress Catalog Card Number: 78-1813

Printed in the United States of America
R-00-2

Library of Congress Cataloging in Publication Data

Dimond, Stuart J.
    Introducing neuropsychology.

    Bibliography: p.
    Includes index.
    1. Neuropsychology. 2. Brain. 3. Mind and
body. I. Title. [DNLM: 1. Psychophysiology.
2. Neurophysiology.   WL103 D582i]
QP360.D55   152   78-1813
ISBN 0-398-03794-9

To Clare and Rebecca

CONTENTS

INTRODUCING
NEUROPSYCHOLOGY

Chapter I

NEUROPSYCHOLOGY: A NEW SCIENCE

What is Neuropsychology?

IF WE want to examine the mysteries of mental life, to know more about ourselves, and to understand the inside workings of the mind we can turn to psychology which is the study of mind and behaviour. Many students are surprized that there is a "science of psychology" and they are even more surprized when they start their courses at the achievement of this subject in the hundred years or so of its history. Who would guess that this vast intangible thing that we call the mind—of which one poet said, "My mind to me a kingdom is" and of which Mark Twain said, "I must have a prodigious quantity of mind; it takes me as much as a week sometimes to make it up."—this kingdom, this great universe can be mapped onto a brain large by comparison to any other brain in nature but infinitely small by comparison to its achievements? Yet this is our job, to hold up the infinitely large mind against the small brain and to try to make the one fit against the other. Where we are successful and the parts fit like a hand into a glove then we say that what results is "neuropsychology." The knowledge of this is the subject of our book.

There are some who say that neuropsychology is the study of our mental functions and our behaviour after the brain has a part missing or a part destroyed, as for example when a surgeon removes a part of the brain or a part of the brain is destroyed by a disease—loss from the brain can and usually does mean a loss from the mind.

Moyra Williams states in her book *Brain Damage and the Mind,* "It has long been recognised that mental functions which cannot be selectively studied under laboratory conditions in the healthy individual may break down in a circumscribed manner as the result of brain injury or disease. Nature herself

3

performs the experiment and its consequences are open to scientific scrutiny. . . . This area has come to be called neuro-psychology."

Edgar Miller in his book *Clinical Neuropsychology* states, "Anything which disrupts the working of the brain or damages its tissues is liable to produce changes in behaviour. The study of these changes often known as 'neuropsychology' enriches our understanding of the mechanisms by which the brain controls behaviour as well as providing information of practical value in the diagnosis and treatment of brain-damaged patients."

Important though this view is it seems to me to be too narrow and somewhat misguided as a definition of what neuropsychology is about, for whilst undoubtedly the study of the person with a damaged brain is an essential pillar, it is not the only support upon which neuropsychology is built.

I believe that neuropsychology is a new branch of science which sets out to actively explain mental life at all of its levels and to discover how this mental life is produced by and related to the structures of the brain. I believe that neuropsychology should grow and develop out of something wider than the study of the brain-damaged person alone. The important thing is the relationship between the brain and what it produces. We are certainly not going to exclude knowledge merely because it comes from somewhere else such as the study of animals with experimental lesions of the brain or the study of the normal person who has his brain in one piece.

Baby, Child, and Man

The brain is the organ of intelligence. It has an effortless accomplishment in guiding and controlling behaviour in everyday life. Whatever may be resolved in the future about the way in which intelligence evolved from primitive forms and the way in which intelligence can be pinned down to parts of the brain fabric, it is certainly the case that coming from out of the brain there is a development of intelligence and that ability flowers and grows providing a testament to the power of the brain to maintain its ceaseless activity, to learn, to profit from experience, and to produce the intellect upon which our lives depend.

Just as a vast mountain range is formed by some massive primeval events in the lost aeons of the history of the earth and as the vast oak is charmed out of the acorn seed, so the mind of man is formed out of the elementary workings of the infant brain. To grow old is an outward and visible sign of an inward and spiritual progression from which the mind of man finally emerges as steel passing through the fire.

The fact is that the brain is active long before the child is born. The quickening of the foetus begins when the child becomes active in the mother's body, and when the baby becomes really active the mother can sometimes be forgiven for thinking that instead of a baby there is a football team in there! Having explored all the possible movements that it can accomplish within the mother's womb, the baby after birth embarks upon a new set of adventures in which, like Alice in Wonderland, it moves on from the discovery of the pattern of one movement to the discovery of the pattern of another as its life unfolds. Despite the fact that the brain is largely wired up for movement, the brain makes one big discovery at this time, perhaps the most important discovery of all, and that is that the brain can tell its body what it wants it to do. In this we see self-will establishing itself and the brain beginning to exercise self-control. Whether or not this is mind over matter is a question we cannot answer at the present time but brain over body it certainly is and the brain engages in a special period of acute mental activity at this time to dominate and bring the body into submission—this we call the period of *learning body control.*

This period of time is one when the turmoil of the baby's activities is gradually, step by step, subjected to the demands of the brain. The activities of the young infant's body are brought under strategic control and this is the dawn of self-awareness. The brain is preoccupied at this stage not only with the problem of what it must do to animate each individual part of the body but also if the will is to be expressed what it must do to make the parts work together so that the body becomes the effective instrument and servant of the brain.

Having accomplished something of this and knowing how the body may be made to work to gratify the brain's need for a servant, the brain, like the great explorers of the Middle Ages having fit themselves out for the voyage, then turns its attention to the world around. Adults frequently fail to realize that the baby is establishing himself as an expert in the practical mechanics of the world. They think that it is a matter of natural cussedness when the baby pulls the tablecloth from the table when the family is in the midst of their meal. They do not realize that this is the baby's way of discovering the natural consequences of his action. The fact is that the baby now enters a stage of *learning about the world*. No one teaches the baby about trigonometry, mechanics, mathematics, or about the principles of action and reaction, no one explains to him the theory of physics or practical mechanics—this he discovers for himself and each baby makes this discovery afresh as his brain grapples with the world around him and the infant comes to some understanding of his place in it. What is this inchoate intuition that the baby acquires so effortlessly, and why does it take six years of classes in school to have explained this thing that every baby knows but none can communicate?

As the feathered fledgling flees from the nest so the baby escapes from the prison of his incoordinated immobility. Like the eagle with strong young wings launching and soaring from the cliff face, the baby burgeons out into the world unknown, but unlike the fledgling supported on a fluid sustaining cushion of air, the baby finds a world which is solid, hard, uncompromising, and capable of dealing that baby a mortal blow. Of course the baby must be protected from the worst of this environment and yet the baby must learn, and so with trepidation on the part of his parents, he explores gradually, bit by bit until he too can navigate fluently and effortlessly like a bird on the wing. What is the baby's brain doing at this time? Something remarkable by any standard—in the great unconscious of the mind that baby comes to a knowledge of the essential mysteries of space and time. The tragedy for knowledge is that the baby can no more articulate these mysteries than can the sea explain the ebb and fall of its tides. Mass, physical form, contour, action and reaction, distance and proximity, the causal relation between events, the texture and three-dimensional structure of the world are things understood in the deepest practical sense by the baby, for that baby remains helpless for only a short while before it becomes the master of its world and enters on a course of destructive annihilation of all valuable objects within its immediate grasp.

There are those who emphasize only the stage when the child begins to speak as the crucial time for the making of the intellect. For them the speaking brain is the intelligent brain. We are in diametrical opposition to this view. The time of learning about the world is the stage when the foundations of creative thinking which distinguish the scientist, the artist, and the man of practical affairs are laid down. Speech has not yet arrived in the compass of the baby's gifts. Speech is not yet used to give communication. Yet the brain already knows how to control the body and now within its destiny it comes to control its world. It is here before the infant can speak that the great foundations of the intellect are laid. It is here that man develops an acquaintance with the knowledge of the world which gives him the understanding—although later he can barely articulate it in words—which later becomes the foundation of all those activities on which our society is based and by which man moulds and shapes the world around him out of the raw plastic of material things.

Whatever might be said about the fertile, seething intellect of the baby before such time as speech is possible, it is still the case that language and beginning to speak has a very special meaning. The baby's first word is greeted by the parent as a new adventure in communication between them. The baby is no great orator but speaking the occasional word gives it a special membership card to the human race. This is the language stage and the brain at this time is intensely active in getting knowledge of language and then in using it as a tool of the intellect.

Many psychologists write books on "language development,"

and what they write about almost invariably is "learning to speak," the time beginning when the child first says something vaguely recognizable as a human word to when the child speaks as well as you or I. These authors usually forget that if you would speak then first you must listen. The infant is a little Hamlet who says, "Give it an understanding but no tongue." He listens but does not speak—indeed he cannot speak but he can listen. How do we know that he listens? We know that he listens in the same way that we know our dog listens. We say something to him and he understands. "Come here, Jane." "Fetch your hat, Simon." "Don't do that, Amanda."—these well used phrases of the English language all show that the baby understands language and furthermore with skill and patient understanding the baby can actually be persuaded by one means or another to carry out commands such as these. The fact is that the baby's brain is used as much for language as for anything else. Long before the baby is mouthing quaint phrases it has listened and it has learned; it has come to understand what people say to it. All this before it is itself capable of stringing words together to make a sentence. Those who suppose that the baby's first word is the beginning of language, and there are many of them, could hardly be more wrong. The fact is that from the earliest point in time the baby is soaking up language like a sponge. We know this because the brain of the new-born baby responds electrically in a special way to language and because the baby demonstrably understands language long before he himself can speak. What he hears creates an imprint upon his brain so powerful that it is never subsequently eradicated.

The time at which the child enters the second stage of language, that of learning to use language, varies quite widely from one infant to another. As soon as he can speak he learns to use the voice at the service of the brain and words become a tool in the quest for self-expression.

It may not have escaped notice that the first words used by babies are the ones useful to them, not the poets words such as contemplation, tranquility, or loveliness but commands such as "up" which means that the baby has to be lifted up, "din-dins" which means that the parent must immediately get the baby's dinner, or "mummy, mummy" which means that the baby thinks it time it had a cuddle whether this be in the middle of the night or whilst his mother is washing the dishes.

The brain has come a long way when that impish thing—the self—tucked away somewhere within the nerve cells and the circuits of the brain starts to use language as the servant of the brain and starts itself out on a career of social manipulation through the power of the spoken word. The brain at this time not only listens to language when other people use it but also it learns how to use its own voice as an instrument to speak, to express the self, but over and above all as something social, as a bridge between that person and the next. It is at this time that the individual begins a social career as something more than a primitive, demanding thing. From then on there follows a rapid development of the skilful use of words.

The strange thing about the power of the intellect is that in addition to these periods of intense activity during infancy the brain achieves a summit of mental function during the periods of middle and late adolescence. The brain works best in callow youth and adolescence not in the athletic vigour of the early adult, the comfort and prosperity of middle age or in the sagacious toothlessness of old age. The fact is that the young person, little more than a child, has a brain functioning better than anything either before or since. The tests which we have available show that at the age of fifteen or sixteen the brain is most intelligent—the summit of the intellect is conquered and from then on there is a slow descent gradually accelerating into decline with increasing age.

Some psychologists express the view which becomes increasingly popular with them as they advance in age that tests of intelligence reflect merely the speed with which the brain reacts to immediate association and that there are realms of wisdom beyond anything so far measured. There may be some truth in this but that which has been measured so far does not show it. Of course it is a matter of concern to us all, in particular to students who depend on their brain power, that we may already be past our peak, having entered into a gradual decline.

Simple Acts and the Brain

We have talked about the intellect and the very highest functions that the brain is called on to perform but we can best see the magnificence and mystery of the accomplishment of the brain when only the simplest acts are considered.

> I will arise now and go to Innisfree
> And a small cabin build there of clay and wattles made;
> Nine bean rows will I have there, a hive for the honey bee
> And live alone in the bee loud glade.

Should we have asked Yeats about his wish to go to Innisfree, his desire to build a cabin, to live in a bee loud glade, we may well have found this to be the totally impractical imagination and anticipation of the poet. Imagination is the great creative force within the brain. The fact is that our mental functions even including imagination are dependent upon our brain at the very highest level, but even simple acts depend upon the brain, those things too simple even to merit a moment's consideration. This morning for example you got out of bed, removed your night-clothes, and dressed ready for the day. You went to the bathroom washed and cleaned your teeth, walked to the kitchen, prepared some breakfast, and made yourself a drink. Before even leaving the house and being barely conscious you have already accomplished a series of the most remarkable routines, breathtaking in their complexity, and yet you do this with hardly a glance, barely a thought for the mechanism of your brain which is doing all this. We can take one very simple examples that of tying shoelaces, we tie our laces almost as an automatic gesture. Our pet dog, intelligent though we may think him to be, cannot tie shoelaces and even the monkey, able though he is, does not have the brain to easily master a skill like this. Our brains are so superb in their efficiency, their activity flows on so smoothly leading us from one task to the next that we do not even realize the nature of the accomplishment. We forget the anguish of the little child that once we were, unable to walk out because our shoelaces were untied. The person whose brain is damaged may sometimes lose this effortless efficiency and may have to learn these simplest of skills all over again. The point to wonder and marvel at is that the human brain can do things of immense complexity and make them seem to us the simplest things in the world.

Mental Ability and Concussion

The interrelationship between brain and mental function is perhaps most clearly illustrated by the decline in mental function when physical damage affects the brain. Many psychological functions, for example, are completely disrupted when there is a massive blow to the brain, and the state known as concussion may result. The building industry has numerous accidents in its list of industrial injuries where concussion features because the person has been hit on the head by an object falling from above, a piece of scaffolding, a piece of masonry, or such.

After the blow the person typically becomes unconscious, then after varying intervals of time he recovers somewhat but is like a person waking from a deep sleep and his mind is disturbed such that he is not in full possession of his faculties. At this time he may be barely aware of what is taking place around him. After the passage of time he may still be dazed and uncomprehending. It is said that he inhabits a *confusional state*. He may fail to recognize his relatives and treat his wife and children as though they were strangers. He may believe that he is at home when in fact he is in the hospital. He may not know that he has had an accident and may remain totally oblivious of the deficiencies of his mental function. He is extremely forgetful and forgets what has been said to him almost as soon as it has been spoken. Gradually the state of confusion begins to clear and the patient regains something of his normal personality. When he gains insight he is well on the way to recovery, but there may well be a gap in his memories of the events leading up to or the time after the accident.

The boxer, of course, is continuously at the mercy of blows to the head. He frequently suffers states of concussion which vary in their severity from one knockout to another. Frequently after a knockout there is complete loss of consciousness with flaccid paralysis and loss of memory for the events before the knockout. Sometimes periods of unconsciousness may be prolonged—the boxer although strangely awake does not know where he is or what he is doing. He behaves as if sleep walking. Gene Tunney, for example, having sustained blows that would floor most people continued to box as if sleep walking. The actions continued although the boxer had no awareness of what he was doing.

That blows to the head damage the brain is well known. Any young person who contemplates a career in boxing or who pursues it, if only as an amateur, should become acquainted with this fact for he is likely to suffer impairment of his abilities. Punch-drunkenness is also something to be acquainted with. As the result of the damage the brain sustains there is a deterioration of skill, slowing of muscular action, uncertainty in equilibrium, and then confusion in the events of everyday life—lapse of memory and a failure of concentration. At a later stage speech becomes thick and hesitating and the boxer gives every appearance of being slightly drunk. Although he talks a lot and he may sing and crack jokes, his mental processes are confused and the ultimate intellectual impairment becomes a severe disablement. There are many examples where the brain when injured exerts only a tenuous hold over the mind and the condition of punch-drunkenness is one of them. Our purpose in talking of the condition is not to dissuade would-be boxers from entering the profession—each person must decide this for himself—but rather to illustrate the way in which the mind touches upon the brain and to show the departure of essential elements of mind after damage has been inflicted upon the brain.

Brain Disease and Mental Ability

Brain diseases are of many types and not all of them are severe but when a person suffers from a severe disease then the progressive loss of mental functions shows very clearly indeed how dependent we are on our brain for the very existence of our mental ability. At first the patient may feel nothing more than hot flushes, occasional headaches, or vertigo, sometimes he may be depressed and sometimes elated. All this is common in perfectly normal people but it becomes exaggerated when a person has an organic brain disease. When the patient begins to behave in an unusual way this is noticed by the family. For example they may sit down to a meal one day to find that the wife or mother has served the pudding before the main course because she has become confused about the correct order. At this stage the afflicted person may forget to dress properly, develop slovenly eating habits, and take little care of personal hygiene. The person begins to forget facts about everday life— whether bills have or have not been paid, whether the clock has been wound, etc.—trivial matters often but contributing immensely to the difficulties of the patient.

Impairment of memory becomes more pronounced. The patient may go into the street and not only forget why he went there but lose himself in local streets as familiar as the back of his own hand. As the disease becomes worse the patient becomes more distractable and less able to concentrate on things. Thinking itself becomes difficult and the patient's activities become more and more limited in scope. At the terminal stage the person is reduced to a vegetative life. Behaviour more resembles that of the infant than that of the adult. Activities are often limited to a few purposeless movements such as stroking the bedcovers, chewing or sucking, grating the teeth, or shaking the head and this represents all that is left of the person's ability and intelligence. The brain is burnt-out although the body may well at this time still be preserved.

The mirror is focussed sharply on the mind of man in these distressing conditions and even more so when deterioration affects the most gifted.

Churchill in 1940 when he was sixty-five years old was appointed prime minister of Great Britain. It was, however, some thirteen years later that a stroke affected the left side of his body, i.e. in the right side of the brain. The doctors were dubious about the part which he could continue to play in public life. Lord Brain said, "If the Prime Minister goes to the party meeting on October 10th he might become emotional or he might get very tired and walk away from the platform badly— or he might even forget what he is meant to say." Churchill, in spite of his stroke, continued his term of office. He was involved in the party conference and much international travel and negotiation, but for much of the time he was a sick man. Paralysis eventually afflicted him, accompanied by the decline of his mental functions. As the years went by he gave up reading. In the latter years he seldom spoke and indeed it was difficult to follow what he said.

Practical Affairs

There are many areas where neuropsychology touches in an important way on practical affairs. The first point is that in neuropsychology we have the development of a new science important to medicine. We have to understand the working of the brain in order that we may know how to deal with disease and disorder as it becomes reflected in the behaviour of man. The second point is that it is here when we consider the relationship of the brain to behaviour that we encounter in an acute form the great moral and philosophical questions about the individual and the place which he holds in society. Here we encounter the questions "What makes me me?" and "What part do 'I' hold in the great social enterprize which is mankind?" The manipulation of the mind, whether this is accomplished through drugs, through neurosurgery, or whatever other means, for medical or for other reasons, is an important part of neuropsychology. How abnormal can that part of me become before someone else with the mandate of society should step in and say that an alteration should take place? Should the individual be allowed to run on unchannelled and unchecked to produce behaviour which society finds intolerable in every way?

To demonstrate the way in which neuropsychology can have a profound influence on practical affairs, we can look at the way people who show abnormal behaviour are treated before the law. Where there exists evidence of brain pathology in association with the behaviour in question then this can be put forward as a defense.

A realisation that physical disease can affect behaviour is seen in the case of Mr. Charlson. Mr Charlson was a devoted and even indulgent father who made a sudden and a savage attack on his son, striking him on the head with a mallet and throwing him from a window. He was charged with various offences against the person and at his trial it was given that there was a possibility that he was suffering from a cerebral tumour. A person afflicted in this way may be liable to an outburst of impulsive violence over which he would have no control. The defendant in this case was entirely acquitted. It was said that he was "acting as an automaton without any real knowledge of what he was doing." The defence of insanity was not raised and the prison medical officer gave evidence that the defendant was sane and not suffering from a disease of the mind. The condition he had and the affliction of his behaviour was attributed to the presence of the cerebral tumour.

This same question arose in a case in which a Mr. Kemp made an entirely motiveless and irrational attack on his wife with a hammer. He was charged with causing grievous bodily harm to her with intent to murder her. It appeared that he suffered from arteriosclerosis which caused a congestion of blood in his brain. As a result he suffered a temporary lapse of consciousness during which he made the attack. It was conceded that he did not know the nature and quality of his act and that he suffered from a defect of reason but it was argued on his behalf that it arose not from any mental disease but purely from a physical one. It was argued that if a physical disease caused the brain cells to degenerate (as in time it might) then, in legal terms, it would be a disease of the mind, but until it did so it was said this temporary interference with the working of the brain was like a concussion or something of that sort and not a disease of the mind.

The strange thing about neuropsychology is that it is leading one to search more and more for abnormalities in the functioning of the brain which cause people to behave in abnormal and sometimes criminal ways. No one says that brain pathology is responsible for everything, nevertheless one is left with a sneaking feeling that our present lack of knowledge is such that many unusual states of behaviour still remain to be associated with pathology or physical anomaly of the brain and that as an article of faith we may believe that covert states underlie much of the behavioural abnormality which is seen. We can hardly blame a man if he behaves in an antisocial way if his brain is taken up with a pathology which disturbs and disrupts his higher mental functions, neither may it be appropriate to punish him for this.

In the case of psychiatric illness, the patient may clearly be disturbed and yet evidence of gross brain pathology may be absent. Yet many psychiatric states give rise to behaviours which are similar in many respects to that where pathology is present. There are categories of psychiatric illness where the suspicion is strongly held that the brain is involved in some crucial abnormal way in producing the disease of the mind, and as neuropsychology advances one can envisage that situation where more and more psychiatric states, although not all of course, come to be related to discoveries of underlying pathology existing in the brain. A number of the major psychiatric categories would perhaps in legal terms be regarded then not as diseases of the mind but the result of interference with the working of the brain. The effect of this would be, as we have seen in the law, that the patient moves to become more in line with people suffering from other diseases, heart complaints, liver disorders, etc. One feels that this change could only be one for the better, resulting in a more tolerant and kindly acceptance of psychiatric illness by the community. There are those who are violently opposed to the viewpoints expressed here, nevertheless it is my opinion that the major practical contribution within the foreseeable future will be in knowledge about psychiatric illness and in the way in which public attitudes to psychiatric states change as a consequence.

For the future there will be a penetration of the mysteries of the brain. The programme must be set up to understand not only the elementary facts of nervous physiology but also the simple and the complex things of which the mind is capable and to determine how the brain functions to produce them both in health and in disease.

It is necessary to digress at this stage to briefly consider the basic structure of the nerve cell, the units making up the nervous system, as well as something of the nervous system itself. It is essential to know something of this as background for the later chapters but the person with a basic knowledge in this area can, if he so wishes, omit reading this section.

Since the invention of the microscope it has been known that the nervous system is composed of small units or cells, these are called *neurons*. The neurons form the cell fabric of the nervous system; they are the individual units whose action provides the groundwork for the workings of the nervous system. Where the bodies of many nerve cells are gathered together the brain has a typical greyish appearance and these parts of the brain are known as the *grey matter*. The body of the neuron usually possesses a characteristic geometrical form. The cell body of the neuron contains a large *nucleus* which contains the genetic material of the cell. Surrounding the nucleus is the *cytoplasm* or protoplasmic substance of the cell body. Embedded in the *cytoplasm* are the *mitochondria,* the oval-shaped structures which provide much of the cell's energy through their capacity to oxidise substances derived from glucose, also the *ribosomes,* the granular substances which fabricate the cell proteins. All this biochemical machinery is housed in a tough membrane composed of a double layer which allows an active transport with external regions but yet at the same time prevents the large molecules and the active substance of the cell from escaping outside.

The nerve cell possesses processes which lead out to contact other cells and it is through these that communication is established. Where large numbers of these processes run together in tracts across the brain they form themselves into bundles of fibres which have a typically white appearance and are known as the *white matter*. The white fibres of the brain can be very long, indeed often many millimetres and in some cases running into centimetres. The processes which lead off from the cells and interconnect to other cells are known as *dendrites*.

Not only are there branching processes which may lead directly from the cell body to contact adjacent cells but so also may there be much longer processes which can lead from the cell body to a more distant source. A long process of this kind is known as an *axon*. The axon, like the dendrites, branches at its end into a number of subprocesses known as the dendritic spines—these are innumerable small processes which lead across through a small gap or *synapse* to make contact with the cell body or dendritic processes of other cells. The axons are themselves coated with a fatty sheath which is responsible for giving them their white appearance.

The neurons are not the only cells of the nervous system and the brain. There is a supporting fabric of cells in the spaces of the nervous system known as the *glia*. This tissue is a special kind of support, but clearly it has other functions as well which remain to be worked out in detail.

The Brain

The most obvious feature of the human brain is the huge *cerebrum* divided down the middle by the midline fissure and composed of the two *cerebral hemispheres*. The surface of the cerebral hemisphere is known as the *cortex*. This is the folded and wrinkled structure so obvious and characteristic of the external surface of the human brain.

The cerebrum can be divided up into the lobes of the cortex. These are the *occipital* at the back of the brain, the temporal at the side and roughly above the ear, the region over the top of this is the *parietal lobe,* and the region at the front at the forehead is the *frontal lobe.* We have already seen that the brain is divided by the midline fissure, but passing between the two cerebral hemispheres is a large wedge of white tissue known as the *corpus callosum* which serves to interconnect the two major regions of the brain.

Lying at the back of the brain are the fist-sized structures of the *cerebellum.* This, like the cerebral cotrex, is a highly convoluted part but the *cerebellum* is in fact separate from the cerebral cortex. The cerebellum is covered with its own cortex and is bilaterally symmetrical at each side of the brain. Generally speaking there is a loss of the coordination of the patterns of fine movements following damage to this region. It is generally assumed that the cerebellum plays a large part in the operation of the control of complex sequences of body movement.

The *midbrain* is the area which lies beneath the cerebral cortex.

The *brain stem* as its name suggests is in fact the stem of the brain. It is an anatomical continuation of the *spinal cord,* the long tract of fibres which runs through the backbone. As the spinal cord runs upwards towards the brain it begins to thicken and then broadens out into the *medulla* and then into the bridge-shaped region or *pons.* It is at this level that the major nerves from the sense organs of the head join themselves into the brain.

Chapter II

THE METHODS OF NEUROPSYCHOLOGY

Introduction

If WE make the claim that neuropsychology is an important new science it will be demanded that we substantiate this claim. One of the ways that we can gain the most information at this stage about the nature of neuropsychology is to look at some of the methods it employs to make fresh discoveries and to gain useful knowledge so that it can advance. If we were to describe some of the findings which form the basis of this science then that would be sufficient in itself, but if we want to understand the subject more fully, to grasp the essential foundations, to penetrate to the very heart of the subject, then we have to study the methods by which it advances and the procedures by which knowledge can be gained. Only then can we become practitioners, have the power to manipulate things, to make discoveries, and to become practising neuropsychologists in our own right.

The kind of world man fashions around himself is determined by the tools he has available. The log cabins of the pioneers were made possible by the invention of the axe. Knowledge likewise comes because there are methods for discovering it. When one studies something as complex as the brain, not only the type of knowledge but the very existence of that knowledge depends on the methods that have been painstakingly and slowly forged for the purpose of developing understanding. Methods are therefore very important, and here we present a survey of methods used for the study of the brain and the part that it plays in producing behaviour and in generating mental life.

The most extensive source of knowledge about the working of the brain is to be gathered from studies where part of the brain has been damaged or removed by neurosurgery. When, for example, a patient has a tumour or part of the brain has been destroyed by a disease, then the surgeon to save the life of that person may well have to remove the diseased part of the brain. The person who has lost part of the brain may well be expected to behave differently from the normal person, and by a study of the loss of ability and the change in mental life and behaviour, we can begin to determine what part the surgically removed structure must play.

The Animal Brain

The study of man in whom some part of the brain has been removed must be regarded as the central focus of our study, the science of neuropsychology. Nevertheless, it is not always easy to make progress and there may be many obstacles to be overcome before research yields its full insights. Not the least of the obstacles is the fact that the investigator depends on nature herself to provide him with his subjects and this she may do once or not at all in the lifetime of the investigator if the condition is particularly rare.

For this and other reasons, it is common to do much work not on man at all but on animals, particularly rats, cats, dogs, and monkeys. In biological science the tradition of studying animals has existed over many years. If a new drug is to be tested, the drug is first given to animals to make sure that it is safe before it is given to man. Where there exists a potential health hazard to man, as in the exploration of space, it is common practice to investigate the effects upon living organisms by exposing animals rather than man to these environments. Animals are also used for convenience, as in genetics, to bring investigations within the bounds of possibility. The span between generations is twenty-five years for man whereas it is less than six months for the rat, and genetic experiments are therefore possible on the rat which are not possible on man. This propensity for rapid breeding, although advantageous, can create problems as happened in a theatre at Frome in Somerset which rapidly became infested with rabbits after a conjurer's rabbits escaped into the stalls. Bunny girls releasing rabbits in London's Hyde Park as a stunt also created a problem because the rabbits bred so quickly that it became necessary to hire a Coldstream Guardsman as a sharpshooter.

Most of the investigations which involve controlled neurosurgery are beyond the bounds of possibility for man even to the most zealous scientific investigator. No person with a healthy brain can have neurosurgery for experimental reasons. Surgeons in the United States who carry out only routine surgical procedures for medical treatment do not go free from the threat of a medical malpractice action. If we wish to have knowledge of the effects of controlled surgical intervention on the normal brain then the study of animals is the only possibility since we cannot think of such surgery for man.

If it is the case that the most important experiments we cannot do, then we may ask how is it ever possible to acquire the knowledge that we seek. In medical research, animal work is done to develop techniques which are later applied to man— heart transplant surgery was developed in dogs. We come, however, to a different principle; the experiments which would give us the greatest knowledge cannot be performed on man at all, and there is no question of the immediate transfer of methods from animal to man. What we are saying, therefore, is that the knowledge obtained from our animal studies must stand in place of that which otherwise would be obtained from man. Animal research, in other words, must fill the gap. If the brain has to be dismantled to find out how it works, then it will be the brain of the rat, the cat, the dog, and the monkey that gives us this knowledge. There are some who say that the human brain has evolved to such an advance degree that any resemblance it may have to lower species is purely superficial. I think that, as elsewhere in medical biology, we can take the view that there is a continuity which touches on all major aspects— change yes but discontinuity no—and that what we are now discovering about the action of the brain of animals is in fact as fundamental a revelation about our own brain as it is about that of lower species. We incorporate within our brain and within our mental life a legacy from our primitive evolutionary history.

The surgical techniques for the study of the animal brain were pioneered by Flourens who removed part of the brain of pigeons and then observed the unusual and bizarre behaviour which they showed. His aim was to discover which parts of the brain are responsible for the behaviour which he observed. Another pioneer investigator was Lashley who studied animal intelligence by teaching rats to run a maze. After the animal had learnt the maze, part of the brain was removed and Lashley tried to find that part of the brain responsible for the learning.

In principle, the basic method of animal neuropsychology is very simple indeed. It is possible to remove part of the brain as Flourens did and then screen the behaviour of the animal for any abnormality, relying on our capacity for basic observation to tell us what the difference now is. The more sophisticated modern technique is to make a measurement of behaviour first. In the studies of Lashley, for example, an animal learns to run a maze; its success or failure is measured by the number of wrong turns it takes as well as the time it takes to get from one end of the maze to the other. The point is that there is an objective measure of behaviour before any surgery occurs. The surgery is then conducted, the appropriate part of the brain is removed, an interval allowed for recovery, and then the animal is tested again on the same tests that it was given before surgery.

In this way an objective assessment is made between behaviour before the surgery and behaviour after the surgery. The facts are there to present as unequivocal evidence to the critic who may wish to dispute the facts as you have discovered them to be.

Although the basic method is simple, it may be necessary to follow a more complicated procedure than this because an animal performing a task on a second occasion can perform better than on the first because it learns the task and improves with practice. We therefore need another group of animals that follow the complete procedure except that they have no surgery and use these animals to show what learning has taken place between the first and second testing. Another group may be included, exposed to the operation and everything connected with it—the anaesthetic, exposure of the brain, replacement of the cranium, etc.—but these animals have no surgery of the brain. Why this group? They are needed to show that the results follow from removal of brain tissue and are not merely a consequence of exposure to anaesthetic, removal of part of the bony structure (the cranium) surrounding the brain, or any other factor of the operation short of the actual removal of brain tissue. In the accompanying table the scheme of work is shown and this includes the three groups: (1) the treated group on whom the brain surgery is performed, (2) the sham group who are operated upon but brain surgery is not performed, and (3) the normal group who carry out the task but have no surgery at all.

Table I

DESIGN FOR THE STUDY OF THE EFFECTS OF
BRAIN LESIONS IN ANIMALS

	Treated Group	*Sham Group*	*Normal Group*
First Testing	Behaviour studied and recorded.	Behaviour studied and recorded.	Behaviour studied and recorded.
Surgery	Part of the brain removed.	Sham operation.	No surgery.
Second Testing	Behaviour studied again.	Behaviour studied again.	Behaviour studied again.
Results	Results of brain removal.	Results of sham operation.	Results of normal performance.

Studies of the Human Brain

We have already seen that by far the greatest effort in neuropsychology is expended on the study of human patients in whom part of the brain has been damaged or removed. As in the study of the working machinery of the animal brain, the principles of study remain the same. The object is to study the human mind and all those things which characterize it—the patient's behaviour, the patient's inner experience and consciousness when the brain is damaged or destroyed—so that we can understand how it is that the brain produces this behaviour, inner experience and consciousness. The aim is to get knowledge of how the brain does the work that it does. If we wanted to know how the frontal lobes (the front part of the brain lying beneath the forehead) work, the technique is to study those patients in whom the frontal lobes have been destroyed through injury or disease and to observe deficiencies in their behaviour. The usual thing is to study not one such patient but a large number, 200 or more cases may be studied. The results are then pooled and the general picture of the defect is taken to indicate a failure in the business of the frontal lobes.

In modern Russian work, for example, patients with frontal lobe damage were studied for their ability with problem solving. The patient had to actually construct cubes according to a given design. These tasks present little difficulty to most normal people but to the person in whom the frontal part of the brain is damaged such tasks present a severe problem. The patients do not allow themselves to be properly oriented to the problems. They frequently enter into the complexity of the problem without proper preparation and they fail to produce an appropriate strategy to come to a solution and this results in typical disorders of performance.

This is typical of the modern study in neuropsychology which looks at some feature of psychological makeup—in this case problem solving— and then works out how the brain produces this by progressively tracking down the parts of the brain involved. The whole realm of mental ability—those features which characterize the human spirit, the deeper mysteries of human consciousness insofar as they are dependent upon the brain—can be studied each and everyone in a similar fashion. Through the neurological clinics of the world pass a progression of patients in whom, taken overall, no one area of the brain is preserved free from the effects of damage or pathology. It follows that in this progression of patients the whole range of psychological functions dependent upon the brain will have been destroyed. The neurological clinic, therefore, forms a natural laboratory for the understanding of the human brain and the production of its mind.

The problem is gaining access to the deeper secrets of the mind and its brain. We are presented with the ultimate Pandora's box, but the methods of contemporary neuropsychology give us a key by which that box may be opened. Fresh possibilities are created by methods which use large numbers of subjects and employ modern statistical techniques to tease out the results. At the present time the march forward is taking place by this route.

There are difficulties of course. These are to be reckoned with but they should not be allowed to stop the forward momentum of our subject. The purity of design of the studies of the animal brain cannot be totally achieved when man is the subject. It is beyond the bounds of question that any surgery, even the most minor, should be performed except for the needs of treatment. Surgery is most often an inevitable thing in the treatment of an illness. Therefore, the research which is conducted has to be viewed against the background of the disease from which the patient suffers.

To overcome these problems, the procedure is not only to study the patient with a damaged brain but also to study other patients who act as controls. The group of patients may be matched with a similar group of normal subjects—matched for sex, age, educational achievement, economic class, or any other variable. Patients in the hospital for brain surgery may be compared with other patients in the same hospital not having brain surgery. Another possibility much employed in contemporary work is to study and make comparison amongst a group of patients with damage to widely different areas of the brain and in this way one group of patients becomes an important control for the other group. Whatever the nature of the discussion of the control procedures, and there are numerous ones to be employed, this method of studying the action of the brain is at the present time one of the most productive avenues of knowledge available to us.

The Single-Case Study

The traditional method by which our subject proceeds is

one incorporated straight out of medicine, where the individual with a gross abnormality is described in great detail as a single case. This is a hallowed procedure. The history of neuropsychology is based on the reported history of patients who displayed interesting and important symptoms associated with damage to the brain, usually of a fairly well-defined kind. This method is usually one of great elegance. It is frequently said in some quarters, by neurologists of the old school, that one single case showing a well-defined lesion is worth more than the collected results of 200 patients with poorly defined lesions.

Something of the importance of the single case as illustrating principles of great significance can be seen in the study by Luria of "the man with a shattered world," the story of a soldier who was injured at the battle of Smolensk in 1943. A bullet penetrated the left side of his brain in an area above the temporal lobes. This patient suffered enormous disabilities. He lost by far the greater part of his memory and although in time some of the memory returned, it still remained very largely impaired. He failed to recall, for example, that he had a mother and two sisters. The memory loss was significant but another feature of this case was even more curious; when the patient Zasetsky attempted to read he could see the strokes which made up the individual letters but he could not combine these strokes to see them as coherent letters, still less could he see the letters as combined words. His disorder was one of combining units into wholes, something which is accomplished effortlessly in everday life. He could not find his way around for although he could see objects separately in his world, he could not ascertain the pattern of their relationship which would enable him to steer his way. In some sense, the ability to make sense of the patterns of the world is a fundamental ability. Presumably this is what the baby does in developing its capacity to gradually interact more and more with the world and it is this capacity which this patient has lost.

Another example is that of a patient of Geschwind in whom the speech area at the left side of the brain had become detached or isolated from the rest of the brain so that although this patient could speak, what she said represented the action of only a tiny proportion of her brain.

A twenty-two-year-old woman admitted to Cushing Veterans Administrative Hospital had been gassed and found in a state of coma with the unlit gas jet of the hot water heater turned on. This patient had suffered extensive carbon-monoxide poisoning and the damage to the brain was typical of such cases. This patient had given every indication of normal functioning intellectually, although perhaps not emotionally, prior to the carbon-monoxide poisoning. When she recovered consciousness, which she did after seventeen days, it was noted that she sang songs and repeated questions. However, on several occasions when the examiner said, "Ask me no questions," she would instead of answering, say, "I'll tell you no lies." Despite the absence of spontaneous speech, it was noticed that she generally repeated phrases spoken to her. Occasionally, however, instead of repeating a phrase, she would complete it in a conventional manner. Thus, as we have already seen to "Ask me no questions," she would reply "Tell me no lies."

Similary she would sometimes complete proverbs or songs. Related to this was the tendency to be induced by the examiner to complete a few phrases. Thus when told, "Close your eyes," she might well say, "Go to sleep." When asked, "Is this a rose?" she might well reply, "Roses are red, violets are blue, sugar is sweet and so are you." To the word coffee, she sometimes said, "I love coffee, I love tea, I love the girls and the girls love me." When singing songs, her articulation of the sounds and her production of melody were correct although she might still substitute the words "dirty bastard" for some of the syllables of the song.

It is obviously a question of the greatest interest to find out what parts of the brain can do when they are detached from the rest. If the conductor of an orchestra suspects the bass clarinet of playing a wrong note he can ask the musician to play alone. Cases of the type described are important in the same way in that they allow the investigator to study the brain as if it were a disassembled motor car, thus a penetration deep into the brain system becomes possible and the dawning of a new insight into the mysteries of the brain can be fostered.

Electrical Activity and the Brain

When we place a hand over the left side of the chest we can feel the heart beating to keep the body alive. The cardiologist can place electrodes on the chest to pick up the electrical activity of the heart. This can then be indelibly captured as a heart-rate trace on the recording instruments. If we place our hands on our heads we cannot feel the brain at work, but the brain like the heart gives out an electrical message that we can capture and record. The message that the brain sends out is like a secret code that we are steadily, but only gradually, beginning to understand. The brain is protected by the bony skull or cranium which makes it extremely difficult to study unless the skull is opened up by surgery. It was an important advance when it was realized that the electrical message of the brain penetrates to the outside and can be studied without opening the skull.

The first discovery of the electrical activity of the brain was made by an English physician, Caton, in 1875. He placed electrodes on the skull or on the exposed brain of rabbits and monkeys and obtained the smallest flickering signal. At that time there was no way of amplifying the signal and it remained as little more than a mere curiosity. Berger in 1929 obtained a steady flickering rhythm at about ten cycles per second from the unexposed human brain. The scientific world was unwilling to accept this finding at that time and it was greeted with almost universal scepticism. When Adrian and Mathews in 1934 used much more sensitive apparatus, the electrical rhythms of the brain were revealed with great clarity.

The subject is first put at ease and then twenty or so electrodes are applied to points on the head. These may be glued on or held in position with a rubber band. They are usually made of silver wetted in a salt solution.

The great technological revolution has been in the the use of amplifiers to make these signals visible to the naked eye and in the use of computers to extract pattern and meaning from them.

The electrical activity of the brain divides up into the following frequencies:

Delta—less than four cycles per second.
Theta—from four cycles to eight cycles per second.
Alpha—from eight cycles to thirteen cycles per second.
Beta—more than thirteen cycles per second.

The dominant rhythm is the alpha which appears at or around ten cycles per second and this is found mostly over the back part of the brain and less frequently over the front part. This rhythm is commonly called the resting rhythm because it occurs when the subject is resting and has his eyes closed. It is cleared away by mental work or when the subject is given mental arithmetic to do or when the subject opens his eyes. As an illustration of the way in which these electrical rhythms can be used to gain a greater understanding of the brain and its activity we can quote studies which show that more intelligent people have the fastest responding brains as measured by the electrical activity. In addition, the severely retarded patient may show electrical activity of the brain which is not far removed from sleep-states. Although the patient is himself awake his brain exists in a semipermanent sleep. We can, therefore, begin to understand the nature of intelligence through the study of "brain waves," and further than this, recent suggestions are that the waves themselves could be used to show the intelligence of the person irrespective of any special training or educational advantage that person may or may not have had.

The electrical activity also reveals when the brain is coming to a decision. A slow wave of negative potential has created interest in recent years. In experiments where the subject has to actively make a decision, this wave appears in the electrical record. It appears to be the brain signalling that the decision has been reached and of course such a thing is fundamental to our understanding of how the brain comes to make decisions.

The electrical activity is also used a great deal to show up fundamental disorders of the brain. If, for example, there is a cancerous growth in one part of the brain, then electrical silence or a distorted wave will exist around that area and so the presence of a brain tumour will be revealed. It is used also in many and various conditions where brain abnormality is suspected, although it may not be possible to tell merely from the behaviour of the patient. Finally, it should be said that all that appears on the record is not necessarily a reflection of the activity of the brain of the patient. Artefacts have to be avoided, one hospital regularly picked up the arrival and departure of ambulances in the courtyard below on its EEG machine.

We have talked about recording the electrical message of the brain but now we have to talk about the reverse of this, i.e. the response of the brain to an electrical message received from outside. Penfield, a famous neurosurgeon, began stimulating the brain with an electrode to find the focus that would trigger off an attack in an epileptic patient, to reveal a focus that could subsequently be removed at surgery. The patient remained conscious during this procedure and it was soon apparent that the behaviour displayed by the patient during this time was capable of telling the investigator a great deal about the working of the brain. Because the patient remained conscious all the time, it was possible for him to describe what was going on in his mind, what his feelings were, and what his experiences were on brain stimulation.

Some of the most interesting work which Penfield conducted concerned the actions of the temporal lobes of the cortex, the region of the side of the brain positioned in the head just above the ears.

The case of NG was reported. She was a young French Canadian woman of sixteen who complained of seizures that were ushered in by hearing a song, a lullaby her mother had often sung to her "Hush-a-bye my Baby." There was often what she called a dream at this stage of her attacks during which she would seem to be in church or in the convent, but always she heard the song.

When stimulation was applied to the right temporal lobe of this patient she said, "I had a dream I wasn't here." The first occasion on which this happened took Penfield by surprise. It became clear that there can be some reactivation of a strip of the record of the stream of consciousness. Points of stimulation in the temporal lobe provide access to the patient's memories which are presumably stored there. Another patient had flashbacks to different times in his life, "I feel as though I were in the bathroom at school." With later stimulation of the same point the patient repeated that he was standing at the corner of Jacob and Washington in South Bend, Indiana. When asked to explain he said that he "seemed to be looking at himself—at a younger age." When the stimulation was repeated the response was quite different. This time he said that he heard music from *Guys and Dolls.* "I was listening to it," he said, "It was like an orchestration."

Another patient described flashbacks from her earlier life under stimulation. They came suddenly whilst at the same time she retained an awareness of her actual surroundings. She gave the following example. "Without warning I seemed to be sitting in the railroad station of a small town, which might be Vanceberg, Kentucky or perhaps Garrison. It is winter and the wind is blowing outside and I am waiting for a train." This apparently was an experience of this patient's life. It was as though the electrical stimulation was opening gates to the dreams and reminiscences of the patient. Was it a chance finding or could the experimenter call out dreams and reminiscences at will? The surgeons talked to the patient for a little while and then reapplied the electrode at the same point without the patient's knowledge. "I hear people coming in, I hear music now, a funny little piece." The patient was describing her experiences but they were not experiences of actual fact. The electrical stimulus to the exposed cortex had triggered the experience. It is clear that these experiences were in the form of hallucinations. Real in every sense to the patient, stemming from the electrical stimulus, but not evident in fact.

Stimulation of the brain in this way has been undertaken as a mapping of the functions of the different parts of the brain and as a method it has indeed revealed many of the most important insights into brain function that we possess at the present day.

The methods described here are considered as representative of the range of possible ones. The panoply of psychology is vast and there is much that it has not been possible to describe or even mention. The final comment I would make is that any of the methods available to current use in psychology can be put to service in the investigation of the processes of the brain and personally I would like to see a much wider use of these methods and some stepping outside of the conventional framework of method choice employed in the past.

Brain and Psychology

We have looked at the brain, at the way that it may be manipulated, and at readouts obtained from it whilst it is in action. If we are to study the brain in relation to the genesis of behaviour and mental processes, it should not be forgotten that not only do we need techniques for investigation of the brain as a physical organ but also we need a corresponding range of skills for the study of behaviour and mental life at an equally sophisticated level. It is not commonly realized that a quiet revolution has taken place in psychology over the past fifty years to provide just this, a sophisticated set of techniques to measure and study nearly all the important varieties of behaviour and mental function. The achievement is considerable and much of the success of contemporary neuropsychology can be traced back to the expertise developed in this area. There is no point in describing in detail here those methods offered by psychology for the study of the actions of the brain. These can be found in any modern textbook on the subject. There are, however, some areas which are of especial importance at the present time and these we shall mention.

One major approach to the study of the capacities of the brain is known as the input/output method. This method means what it says, the brain is given some input and what it does with it is studied as the output and comparison is made between what goes in and what comes out.

A person may, for example, visit a cinema and sit through a film. If afterwards we were to ask that person about the film we should most likely find that he remembered most of the major happenings of the film, but at the same time many small points of detail and even some of the major episodes may well be forgotten. The person also may actually make up facts about the film that are untrue or add and interpret in a way which is inventive perhaps but inaccurate. The point to be stressed is this, we can understand something of the brain as it acts by giving the person material to be viewed (input), and then we diagnose how successfully the brain has worked upon this. The subject is tested afterwards to see how much he can recall (output). By making a comparison of what the subject sees (the input) and what the subject says he saw (the output) we assess the capacity of the brain to transmit information through its systems. At the same time we can discover the ability of the brain to reconstruct, to invent, or to simply be wrong by the study of the contributions it makes which had no place in the material originally presented to it.

As another example, we can quote studies of learning to type. The skilled typist reads the material that is before her or listens to that relayed to her over headphones. The message she receives goes to her brain and there it gets translated into the deft, quick, and effective muscular movements of her fingers which tap out the message quickly and with the greatest accuracy. In other words, the brain of the typist is acting as an information transmitting system. As the typist acquires skill she becomes more effective as a transmitter of information. At typing school, the skill of the typist is measured by a check comparing what is to be typed with what acutally appears as typing from her fingers.

This technique forms the basis of much research in neuropsychology, where to study the functions of the brain, both in health and disease, it is important to know how effective it is as a transmitter of information.

Another set of techniques available to the psychologist and of particular use in the neurological clinic are those which measure aptitude, personality and intelligence. The psychologist has before him an armament of techniques and skills to be used to study the effects of damage to the brain. These techniques are widely used to contribute to our knowledge of disorder as it affects the brain.

It frequently falls to the psychologist to test those aptitudes which remain after the person has been ill and perhaps suffered some disorder affecting his brain. This is done to find out if the person's work skills have been affected, whether he can return to the same work, or if not, what abilities he has that he can develop and use. Aptitudes can be regarded as special skills. One person may develop a special skill for playing the piano; another person may never develop this skill. Aptitudes are not the same thing as general intelligence, although they may bear some relationship to it.

Personality may be regarded as those characteristics of behaviour and mental life which distinguish the individual and make him what he is. Techniques are available to measure different aspects of personality, or the "traits" of the person as they are known, although it is fair to say that the measurement of personality is something that is still in its infancy. This remains one of the most important problems to tackle in the future because we need to know how the unique as well as the general qualities of each individual are related to the unique and general features of that individual's brain. This is important because we need to know how a person's personality is changed after he has had surgery upon the brain, and we need to know those parts of the brain which, when damaged, produce the most profound and deleterious changes in personality so that interference with these areas can be avoided if at all possible.

Intelligence tests are widely used to reveal mental impairment where such exists. The Wechsler Intelligence Test is commonly used for this purpose. The mental stature of each person is assessed by comparison against the score of many thousands of individuals of his own age. His score becomes the intelligence quotient or IQ. The average IQ is placed at a hundred. People who are more intelligent score higher than this, people who are less intelligent score lower.

The different levels of intelligence are as follows:

	IQ Range
Subnormal—Idiot	Below 25
Imbecile	25-50

	IQ Range
Subnormal—Moron	50-70
Borderline Subnormal	70-80
Low Normal	80-90
Normal	90-100
High Average	110-120
Superior	120-140
Very Superior	Above 140

The Wechsler test is divided up into a number of subtests which include such items as Comprehension, Arithmetic, Digit Span, and Block Design. This test is frequently employed as a test of brain damage because some of these involve well-established habits or skills and maintain their level in spite of damage whereas other items may well be more severely affected.

In addition to tests of general intelligence, there are also tests designed specifically for the clinic to reveal mental impairment where such exists. Often these are special forms of intelligence tests.

The Hunt Minnesota Test was designed specifically to evaluate organic brain damage. The vocabulary part of this test is relatively stable, holding up in the face of the general deterioration of the rest of the functions of the brain. The patient is tested with a list of words which require definition. His score on this test most reflects undeteriorated performance against which the results on the other tests, expected to show deterioration, can be compared.

There are in addition many other types of tests which are aimed at studying the action of specific brain parts. The study of what each hand can do is, for example, generally taken to reflect the capacities of the cerebral hemispheres at each side of the brain. From the fact that the vast majority of the population are right-handed and from the fact that the right hand in such people is used for writing and self-expression, has come the idea that the side of the brain controlling the right hand must be dominant over its partner on the other side. It is not only a question of writing; in boxing, one hand, the preferred hand, gets used as the aggressive weapon. The specialisms of the two halves of the brain appear, therefore, to stretch back into the very early history of man when his very survival was involved, and the organization of man's brain as we know it today was shaped by those very powerful primitive forces which supported his survival.

The facility of the two sides of the brain can also be explored by special techniques which implant information at one or the other hemisphere. In our own work, for example, we have found a way of testing each half of the brain for damage. A signal flashed into the left visual field goes to the right half of the brain, a signal in the right visual field goes to the left half. By flashing messages to the two sides of the brain we can compare their performance. If one side is damaged by a tumour, a blood clot, or some other type of pathology then when we compare the two sides we find that the performance on the damaged side is at a very low level indeed, whereas the other side may be unimpaired. In this way, it is possible by comparing the two sides of the brain to find damage that exists there and which may otherwise pass unnoticed.

This principle has been exploited in tests of dichotic listening, which is a method to assess the contribution of the parts of the brain to the listening process. Here, each ear receives its own tape-recorded message but both ears receive a message played at the same time. The subject cannot adequately follow two messages at the same time and the person resolves the dilemma of choice by selecting one message rather than the other. One side of the brain is more effective at receiving a message than is the other. One of the major findings using this method is that the right ear (left hemisphere) is more effective when it comes to receiving speech messages and the left hemisphere has an advantage for speech processing, but the left ear (right hemisphere) is superior for music and possibly for other types of sound as well.

Chapter III

SOME FUNDAMENTAL BRAIN SYSTEMS

Introduction

F ROM ancient times a dichotomy has existed in man's thought about the nature of his very being. A division has been made between the higher aspects of life—those factors we think of as rational and intellectual, distinguished by the higher realms of consciousness—and the lower less differentiated part of our makeup concerned with the irrational and emotional parts of our life. Freud, for example, distinguished between the "ego," the more rational volitional aspect that we have already described, and the "id," which contains everything that is inherited and remains fixed in the constitution, representing the blind impulsive forces of the personality. The strivings of the "id" were described as largely sexual both in the narrower and the wider sphere.

The tendency has been to regard the brain as also divided up into two separate compartments—the higher brain with its capacity for rational thought, intellect, and will, and the lower brain, sharing something in common with the forces that motivate the behaviour of animals but concerned essentially with the springs of motive force and those primitive instincts which represent the blind impulsive strivings of the personality leading the individual towards aggression and the destructive forces of individual conduct.

Although in broad terms this picture of the relationship of psychological functions to the workings of the brain may not be so far from the truth, nonetheless it may be naïve to divide up the functions of the brain in this artificial way. The brain does not in reality exist as two separate compartments—a higher and a lower one—nor is there an obvious separation between what is described as the higher and lower attributes of the behavior of man.

38

The fact is that the so-called lower parts of the brain are indispensable to the full functioning of human abilities at whatever level they are expressed. These parts of the working of the brain which we call fundamental as brain mechanisms, and will describe in somewhat more detail, are as essential to that which makes men human as are those parts concerned with his rational and intellectual life. The fact is that conscious activity is shot through with interpenetrating strands which owe no direct allegiance to rational and intellectual action but which nonetheless give behaviour a characteristic quality which enhances rather than diminishes the nature of man. There is a working machinery of the brain which underpins the highest intellectual function but that machinery adds its own voice and its own characteristic imprint to the capacities of man.

We must assume that there is a capacity for intercommunication between the different regions of the brain. Each part has a significant role to play and we may not at present safely assume that any one brain part dictates to another, and we may not as yet be in a position to specify the chain of command as it operates in the brain. Ascription of the terms higher and lower can also be misleading because what may be regarded as a higher function in one sense need not be so regarded in another. The skill, coordination, and equilibrium achieved by the acrobat may be regarded as remarkable for the display of the finer aspects of muscular control. Viewed against this background, it must be seen as one of the highest accomplishments that man can arrive at by intensive training. Yet if the very best human acrobats were to be compared with monkeys in their coordination and agility, or for that matter with the bird correcting gracefully during its flight, we would be unable to regard the performance of man as in the highest category.

In addition, evidence of a substantial kind exists that the lower parts of the brain play a major part in what must be considered to be the highest functions—for example, the expression of the emotions, the facility of communication, and consciousness itself—at the same time the upper reaches of the brain are equally as certainly involved in some of the more mundane aspects of function. Despite these cautions, some

parts of the brain do contain systems which are more fundamental than others in that they are basic to psychological functions as well as to the very existence, survival, and integrity of
the individual.

The Brain and Capacity for Survival

It is clear that one has to think of the brain not only as an
instrument commanding and determining those things which
we do but also as an organ, the possession of which allowed
man to survive during the period of his primeval past, and as
something which endowed him with the resilience to survive
his encounters with a hostile environment. The evolutionary
premium given because the brain is fashioned in the way that it
is, provided man not only with the resilience to survive and to
perpetuate his species but also to achieve an evolutionary su-
premacy which enabled him to transcend all other animal
forms to become the most complicated and advanced representative of the process of evolutionary development.

The brain of man has developed unique from everything
which went before, although it arose from the mammalian
prototype to which it has a close and fundamental relationship.
The brain of man could be said to have advanced because of
two important factors. In the first place there is a toughness
and a resilience in structure which gives it the capacity to keep
the life processes going and to regulate them with great precision and reliability—"the very heart of the machine." The
second factor was the plasticity and modifiability of some parts
of the brain which allowed for the evolution of creative intelligence, which must be accounted the crowning, if not the final,
achievement of evolution in action.

It goes without saying that man's psychological functions do
not stand outside of the forces of evolution. Those aspects of
his makeup which acted back upon his environment—his conceptions of primitive science where accurate, his capacity for
magic and ritual insofar as these concerned the germs of truth
about how things actually are—all fostered survival because
they allowed him to exert control over his life and to insulate

himself from the forces of environmental hostility. Intelligence was self-protective and acted reflexively through the capacity for survival, not only to sustain itself but also to encourage more profound and deeper forms of brain action which gave man an even stronger grasp upon the world.

The forces of evolution acted upon structure and form. They also acted upon patterns of behaviour of a stereotyped and fixed nature passed on by the genetic mechanisms from one generation to another. The forces of evolution also acted upon all aspects of conduct which gave man an edge over his rivals in the classic natural drama; here we must include the qualities of the senses, the capacity for sustained action, the ability to learn and to profit from experience, the patterns of ritualistic and moral behaviour, the desire and the ability to fulfil plans for concerted action, and the capacity to live an ordered life in which social integration is at least as important as social destruction. The higher reaches of man's mind have been shaped by the process of evolution as has the nature of his skin and the pattern of the distribution of hair upon his body.

However, the flowering of human abilities occurred because the brain itself was already a tough resilient vehicle capable of carrying the burden of genetic and mutatory experiment without at the same time showing any breakdown in its capacity to sustain life and promote the survival of the species.

Indeed it could be said that the finest achievements of the brain were possible only because one part of the brain continued in a relatively unmodified state to keep a tenacious grip over those processes which make life possible, at the same time permitting exploration by other parts to enable them to reach out, to grasp, and then to preserve within their structure that thing that we call intelligence.

The abilities with which man is endowed are not therefore simply those of elevated intelligence, but deep within his brain is a core or fabric which controls the basic machinery of his life and in all probability it is this which he shares most in common with the rest of the vertebrate creation. How far this fundamental core of man's being can be said to extend its boundaries and insidiously infiltrate its functions upwards into

higher mental action is a matter for debate. The brain is only
partly created anew at each stage of evolution the hulk remains
much the same although the superstructure is modified. However, even if the basic hulk of the brain remains totally unchanged and if complicated functions are superimposed, not
added like one apple on top of another in a basket but inter-
meshed with the life mechanisms which already exist, then
some rearrangement of and integration with the pre-existing
networks may be essential. It does seem that man is in receipt of
a part of his brain which has been modified only little in its
recent history, and that it was this very capacity of the basic
unit to remain preserved and to complete its essential functions
which freed the rest of the brain for experiments in the evolution of creative intelligence enabling man to occupy the position that he does. This is the primitive brain, the archaic brain,
the seat of the barbaric emotions so essential to the survival of
the individual and the species.

The area which regulates the basic life processes in the brain
of man is the brain stem. As its name suggests, this is the
"stalk" part of the brain which exists as a continuation of the
spinal cord. Within it lie the life maintaining system and centres for respiration—those parts which ensure that the individual breathes properly, those parts which ensure the activity
of his heart, and those parts which ensure that other bodily
functions are regulated in a smooth and efficient manner.

Although such systems bear a relationship to the rest of the
brain, the individual in which the higher centres have been
destroyed through disease or injury may still, if the brain stem
regions are preserved intact, continue to live, although at a
vegetative level and one in which there is, of course, little in the
way of conscious mental action in the sense in which we understand it. If tumours or other pathological states develop in this
region, then damage to the brain stem can pose an immediate
and serious threat to the life of the individual. In addition to
disturbances of motor and muscle activity, there are disorders of
respiration and general failures of the vital systems by which
human function continues and by which it is maintained.
There may well be a rapid downward course ending in the

death of the patient. The early signs of damage to this region include some impairment of the processes of consciousness, the degree of which varies considerably, soon the patient loses consciousness, and then follows the decline of vital functions.

It seems clear from this that there are mechanisms in the brain stem essential to life. Without these mechanisms it is impossible for the individual to survive. Yet the fact must be mentioned that these essential units are not without some connection to the higher reaches of the brain. Whilst the mechanisms we have described might best be classed as automatisms, they are nonetheless somewhat susceptible to influences from other parts of the brain. We have come to a knowledge in recent years that the functions even of these vital processes can be modified under the influence of learning and that the fundamental mechanisms are responsive within limits to commands from elsewhere in the brain, although at the same time it must be said that the hold which the higher brain exercises is a tenuous one and one which is not always easy to establish.

Wakefulness and Alerting Mechanisms

There is a primitive core to the brain which acts to allow the individual to survive. This is not however all there is to the archaic brain. Situated in the same part of the brain as these life-regulating mechanisms are systems which act not to preserve the continuous automata of life but to regulate the activity of the individual on a rather different basis. These are centres which control sleep and wakefulness. These centres form part of an alerting system stretching upwards into the brain and also part of one extending downwards to influence the mechanisms of the body. They are strategically placed and it is this placement which may account for their incorporation within the brain stem. The system which controls wakefulness—situated in the brain stem, is described as the reticular system because of its netlike structure. From this system, nerve fibres run upwards to the topmost parts of the brain to wake up this part of the brain, to bring it into a state of readiness to receive messages and to perform its work. It works like an early morning telephone call which alerts the individual and sets him upon his course for the day. In other words, it is a system preprogrammed to alert the individual, at those times when this is necessary, to a glad confident morning. Not only does the reticular system work upwards for its function of promoting wakefulness, but also it works downwards into the lower parts of the nervous system, to the motor and reflex mechanisms deep down in the spinal cord.

This facility to activate played a special part in the evolution of the brain. It occurs in close proximity to the life-maintaining centres of the brain. It is a primitive and archaic system in phylogenetic history.

Alerting is not, however, something confined to the question of whether the organism remains asleep or awake. The fact is that the action of this system is to change the whole relationship which the individual holds to the environment. Before alerting takes place, the individual may have been quiet and unresponsive or even stuporous, but after activation has taken place the individual enters a different reactive relationship with its world. It becomes sensitive to the smallest signal and develops activity where none existed. The individual cannot maintain states of high activation over long periods of time for physiological reasons; high states of activation occurring at times when the individual is not confronted with danger or threat are inappropriate and could set the individual at a disadvantage. They would interfere with feeding or other types of activity essential to the maintenance of life.

It seems therefore that the systems of activation eventuated at an early stage in association with the primitive life-sustaining parts of the brain because they served a purpose in promoting the life and success of the individual. If, for example, the individual can show highly intense activity at those times when danger especially threatens, then this may well increase its chance of survival and allow it to escape. The situation is one which fits the need very much like that described by Groucho Marx when he asked Harpo the shape of the world. Harpo (he had not yet turned exclusively to pantomine) said candidly that he did not know. Whereupon Groucho gave him a hint:

"What," he asked, "is the shape of my cuff buttons?"

"Square," said Harpo.

"I mean the cuff buttons I wear on Sunday—not every day. Now! What is the shape of the world?"

"Round on Sunday, square on weekdays." replied Harpo who shortly afterwards took his vow of professional silence.

Activation means not only a greater working of the muscles and the nerves but also it alerts the senses and brings them into more efficient use. The individual is reflexively more alert to the danger to its survival which exists and this in turn will bring on the activity patterns likely to lead it to escape from danger.

The activating system provides a brighter sensory input at times of special need and increased movement, perhaps diffuse and random but more intense at those times of danger. The organism has a slight edge in its fight for survival but an edge nonetheless which allowed it to take an important first step in organising the brain along modern lines.

Out of this system, which intrudes alertness into an otherwise tranquil state, developed the control over rhythmic, circadian activities and the cycles of sleep and wakefulness which characterise much of the behaviour of the higher animals and particularly of man. The possible evolutionary significance of sleep is that it could be seen as something which allows rehabilitation of much of the body function. It represents a time when much of the action is in fact shutdown, despite the fact that movements are still to be observed during sleep. It also represents a time when there is a limiting of the processes of sensory input, and in this sense is a stage of comparative quiescence. It seems, however, that the tendency for the activating system to move from a sporadic externally controlled firing to internally controlled cycles of regular action is something which occurs relatively late in evolution.

If the system controlling alertness should be damaged by a lesion within the brain stem or in some of the associated systems then the individual may well show a loss of the electrical signs of alertness within the brain and he may fall into a profound sleep from which it is impossible to arouse him. Those cases in which damage to the brain causes the person to lose consciousness are almost invariably those in which there is damage affecting the functions of the brain stem and the system we have described. It is seldom the case that there is an outright loss of consciousness when individuals have head injuries to other parts of the brain. It has been suggested that the brain stem is involved in monitoring and maintaining conscious states.

The effects of damage to these areas are seen when tumours (cancerous growths) develop in the different regions of the lower parts of the brain. The person who has a tumour will suffer from short intermittent attacks of deep unconsciousness usually followed by quick alertations of breathing, irregular pulse, and fluctuations of blood pressure, together with increased tension of the limbs—disorders which frequently having pursued a severe course, result in death. If a tumour exists at a higher part in the brain, but still in the subcortical regions, then the patient can enter a state more like sleep. In cases such as these, the waking systems of the brain are involved and the growth of a cancerous body in this area of the brain disturbs their functions to a greater or lesser degree depending upon the position in which they are situated. Certainly these cases, in which there is clear-cut damage, illustrate the importance of this area for maintaining sleep and wakefulness and illustrate the fact that such systems exert a general effect upon the overall action of the brain.

Some surprise may be occasioned by the fact that the locus we have so far described should be situated in the stem of the brain and not at the highest levels where the most advanced functions reside. This very question illustrates an immediate and difficult problem. Activities at one part of the brain can have an influence over other parts even though they are far distant. Their function is that of remote control or that of a distant switch calling activities into operation and though taking no direct part in the mechanism itself forming an integral part in the circuit of control. Some pundits would argue that as long as we continue to accept that there might be circuits of remote control acting in the brain—as a thermostat switch may control a central heating system or a time switch turn streetlights on and off—then we may never understand fully the workings of the brain. We are not able to say that damage to one area actually destroys the mechanisms of function itself but problems may represent ready interference with one of these more remote controlling circuits. The fact that we may at first be unable to locate the actual mechanism does not mean that in the future this will not be possible. At present, we may need to be cautious so as not to confuse a remote controller for the heavy machinery of the brain itself, for damage to each may have equivalent effects upon the capacity of the individual to function.

In the case of these systems which act to alert and activate the brain we must beware of the assumption that they are necessarily the seat of consciousness. The analogy with the remote control switch is appropriate—it is the system which wakes up the brain and calls it into action for a given temporal period or makes provision for it to be especially on the alert. The suggestion is that in defining this system, we do not necessarily describe at the same time the means by which conscious decisions are produced. The field-marshall may be woken by his batman each day. The batman may prepare the field-marshall for especially important meetings or particularly difficult engagements but the functions of the batman are not the same as those of the field-marshall, although the field-marshall's efficiency may well be impaired as the result of the failings on the part of his aide.

The view should perhaps be expressed that the systems we have so far described, as far as consciousness are concerned, are the ones which open up the actions of the brain or shut it down. The opening up or the closing down may not, however, of itself represent the fabric of consciousness but merely a limiting constraint—one necessary feature in order that conscious functions can occur and be expressed outwardly in behaviour.

Emotional Conduct

We have described those features which lie at the very core of the mechanism of the brain and which through their integrity sustain and preserve the life forces or form the very fabric and mechanisms for life. As the ancients regarded the heart as the core of man's being, so we would regard the stem of the brain as such.

The first prerequisite consisted of the organisation of a system to sustain life. Much of the work of evolution directed itself to the strengthening of the internal organisation for animate life and in providing resilience in those systems so formed. With regard to the question of survival, however, the factors of internal organisation lead the individual only part of the way towards reliable perpetuation of the species. It is not sufficient for the brain to evolve as a mechanism of great internal strength and resilience, if at the same time the members of the species fall prey continually to factors outside which destroy the individual despite the strength of its internal organisation. There has to be something more than a simple and efficient but intrinsic mechanism for the regulation of life. It is necessary to shelter the life mechanisms from the storms which come from outside. Sexual behaviour propagates the species but also the individual creates a protective mantle of fear and timidity to facilitate its survival. Here we witness a new principle at work, that of emotion conceived as the means by which the individual interacts with the world. Emotion is first an outgoing principle towards the creation of the race, the perpetuation of it through sexual reproduction, but secondly an essential force which promotes survival through patterns of aversive behaviour such as those of aggression, timidity, and fear.

The emergence of emotion takes place early in evolution. It too is something related to the organisation of relatively primitive parts of the brain.

There is a core of the brain responsible for emotion which includes parts of the brain stem, the primitive olfactory part of the brain, some parts which lie above the brain stem including the hypothalamus, stretching upwards into the sides of the cerebral hemispheres, the amygdala which we shall discuss in a later chapter, and other related structures which form the limbic system.

However, we can illustrate something of the function of these areas by reference to the action of one part of it—the hypothalamus. This is a collection of nerve bodies which has its physical location at the base of the forebrain. Although the hypothalamus is very complex, it is nonetheless a small area which remains relatively unchanged in its anatomical construction in ascent through the mammalian groups, including man. This gives confidence that much of what we know about the action of the hypothalamus from animals, and a great deal is known, may also be largely true for man. The many functions of the hypothalamus have been described in detail by other writers (Rose 1973 for example). It plays an integral part in the regulation of the hormone system of the body and as the result of this, damage to the hypothalamus can cause diabetes shown in the consumption of large quantities of water (diabetes insipidus). In addition, it contains homeostatic regulatory systems concerned with the regulation of body temperature, with the mechanisms for eating and drinking, as well as mechanisms for participation in the limbic functions for control of emotion, rage, aggression, fear, and sexual behaviour.

The hypothalamus contains a set of basic mechanisms which regulate body temperature, food intake, and water intake. Where damage to the hypothalamus exists these may break down. Temperature regulation becomes difficult or proceeds in an abnormal direction. This in turn triggers abnormal responses of panting, sweating, etc. in attempts to compensate. The individual also may lose control over the regulation of feeding and drinking behaviour. Overeating can develop and reports exist of excessive obesity in cases where there is known hypothalamic damage.

To the neuropsychologist, the part played by the hypothalamus in the control of rage, anger, and aggression is equally important, if not more so. The demonstration that fundamental patterns of emotional behaviour can be laid down in specific regions of the brain is a fact of enormous consequence both with regard to a theoretical understanding of the brain and in the clinical prospect of treatment for abnormal emotional and behavioural conditions.

Not only is it the case that organisms show exceedingly aggressive behaviour when the hypothalamus is stimulated but so also do individuals in whom the cortex is surgically removed or destroyed. In the decorticate animal the hypothalamus, released from its higher centres of control, leads the individual to become exceptionally aggressive and to show symptoms of intense rage, or sham rage as it is known. The hypothalamus also plays a part in the regulation of sexual behaviour in both male and female animals as shown by electrical stimulation of the hypothalmic areas.

Although much sexual behaviour can be regulated in areas of the nervous system below the hypothalamus—male humans and animals whose brains have been severed at the spinal cord will still respond to genital stimulation with erection and ejaculation—nonetheless the whole pattern of sexual behaviour is considerably more complex than this suggests, involving as it does emotional states of readiness brought about by hormone control. Interesting information has accumulated of the direct interrelation of sex hormones with the hypothalamus, if the former are injected in this site or pellets implanted into the brain at the hypothalamic region then animals may well be induced to show advanced sexual function as a result.

That something of these same effects are to be observed in man is evidenced from case reports which describe behaviour when there is known damage to the hypothalamic systems. Patients report sexual feelings of an episodic nature in conjunction with hypothalamic damage from a tumour. Not only do patients report feelings of abnormal sexual intensity but also they show most of the other hypothalamic disorders as well.

Frequently patients show disorders of eating and drinking as well as volatile behaviour including rage and uncoordinated aggression. Some of the hypothalamic condition appears to be well represented in man and we may suspect that we are coming to a picture of hypothalamic function accurate in at least some respects as concerning its function within the total complex of the brain.

On the Nature of Motor Function

If we were to ask why should a brain be necessary in the first place, then we would have to argue that the need for such an organ arose not only because of the essential life sustaining principles and the need to control, govern, protect, and stabilise the mechanisms associated with them, we would also have to argue that a defining feature of animal life is that movement is shown and that this occurs in abundance. This very facility for movement, at once so characteristic and complex when it advances beyond the state of uncoordinated or random activity, presupposes by its very existence mechanisms of control and coordination which we know the typical brain and nervous system to possess. If the moving animal had no brain then evolution would invent one. The fact is that as soon as organisms cease to occupy a stationary mode of life and proceed by intricate movements then complex neural structures are essential to effect control.

Movement is not usually the result of uncoordinated contraction and expansion of the muscles, although movement can be achieved by these means, it is more often a progression achieved by an orderly flow of activity between sequences of muscle groups each taking a share in the action, each making their own contribution according to a highly organised and elaborate plan. The fact is that the body of man is clothed not only by skin but also by a layer of muscles each anchored in certain directions, each contracting in its own specific location. It is as if the body itself is wrapped around with layer upon layer of muscle fabric. It is this mantle of interlocking forces and interweaving tensions which provides the human body with the flexibility and sensitivity in the performance of its everyday actions which it undoubtedly possesses. But this vast interweaving fabric would be rendered useless and fall into chaos were it not for the brain and nervous system which animates it and calls it into working activity. The brain and nervous system play upon this system of body muscles in calling it into action to characterise that which we do. The brain and nervous system, in working out their actions upon the muscles, provide man with an extensive range, limited in some ways but almost unlimited in others, of motor patterns and synergies coordinated into smooth flowing assemblies which through their action allow him to express the complexity of his being.

The brain is more than this however. The smooth flowing but occasionally turbulent muscle synergies of the body are the means by which the brain exerts the forces of its action in life, the mode for it to realize its plans "to breathe into the machine." In a sense, therefore, what we consider is the executive machinery responsible for the behaviour we show, yet at the same time it has to be remembered that executive machinery itself implies the necessity for still higher systems to control it.

Some of the basic patterns of body movement are controlled in fact not only by the brain but by the spinal cord and the lower centres of the nervous system. There are patterns of *reflex actions*. There are numerous examples of these, e.g. the kicking of the leg when the patient is tested in the surgery by the use of the traditional knee jerk. If the tendons are smartly tapped with a hammer on the crossed knee, then signals are dispatched straightaway to the spinal cord and messages get returned to the muscles which then cause the leg to jerk. Reflex systems exist for the promotion of the rapid defensive actions of the body but they also exist for the balance, control of postural mechanisms, and compensatory reactions of the body caused by movements of the legs.

The reflex equipment, as we have seen, acts as a kind of remote station largely within the spinal cord for the control of the actions of the body. The individual in whom the upper reaches of the brain has been severely damaged or temporarily suspended by the use of powerful drugs may well show patterns of movement, largely of a slow, rolling, disordered kind, exercised under the control of the spinal cord. Patients may also develop a state of *decerebrate rigidity* in which the spinal cord released from the control of higher brain centres triggers its reflex actions to their maximum extent resulting in stretching the limbs and rendering the patients stiff and inflexible.

The point which we wish to emphasise is that a whole variety of complex motor control systems exist in man which are laid down at a lower level of the nervous system than the brain, the feature of these reflexes is their largely automatic nature. Such systems are nonetheless brought under control by the modifying influences of higher brain control and pathways stretch upwards in rich supply to the controlling centres located in the brain itself.

One of the systems of the brain which exerts a profound effect upon the control of the motor behaviour is that of the cerebellum. This is a part of the brain connected to the rest but yet identifiable as a separate unit from it.

The cerebellum is a much folded and convoluted structure which lies towards the back of the brain. It consists of a convoluted skin covering an interior of white matter. The cerebellum appears to play a large part in the control of motor movements. It may well be that the cerebellum is intimately concerned with the capacity to learn patterns of motor movements and of disentangling the patterns of action necessary for complex control.

If there should be a damage to the cerebellum, there is severe disruption in the coordinated patterns of the motor movement. For example, a patient suffering from a disorder of the cerebellum may well not be able to reach out to grasp an object efficiently. It may well be impossible for the patient to bring two hands together in a coordinating relationship. There may be fine and gross tremors associated with resting periods as well as other gross disorders of body movement. Despite the importance of the cerebellum in the control of motor movements, it is still the case that much of the responsibility of the control and volition of planned motor movements resides with the cortex—the most recent evolutionary achievement of the brain and the centre for the highest of mental functions—which we describe in detail in the next chapter.

By the use of the techniques of brain stimulation and by the study of patients in which damage has occurred at these highest motor areas, it has been possible to map out some of the functions of the brain involved with the control of motor movement. The regions of the brain at the higher centres concerned with the motor output are known as the areas of motor cortex. Penfield provided a map of the motor cortex by stimulating parts of the motor areas of the brain electronically and then observing which parts respond to such stimulation.

One of the most pervasive features with which animate organisms including man is endowed, is a logic of body action which involves highly coordinated patterns of muscle movement each under control, each coordinated with others into complex synergies of function, each synergy following a sequential arrangement or coordinated plan. It is clear that organisms become endowed with this aspect of their functions from an early point indeed and that from that point onwards one of the jobs of the programme presented to the brain is to control and elaborate these complex actions.

There is no doubt that as types of movement become progressively more intricate during the course of evolution, the patterns for control to take place also have to be correspondingly more elaborate. When the nervous system found itself leading the field in the design of arrangements to make motor movement possible, a system of logic became necessary which could allow the animal to move forward successfully without great difficulty and a system furthermore which although automatic in some respects could compensate for changes, as for example, a bird alters flight patterns in the face of a strong wind.

It is probably true to say that the logic by which the brain solves its problems concerning the control of motor action remains one of the deepest mysteries, yet in some respects, it appears to be one capable of most immediately yielding up its secrets. Certainly much of the force of evolution as it acted upon the brain must have been concerned with the level of efficiency, in determining the adroitness and skill of its action, which the logic of the brain imparted to the organism. The more skilful animal would be the more successful in using the power of its limbs efficiently and working to programme its actions effectively, such an individual would inevitably be the one with the evolutionary advantage. The problem of the logic of the nervous system is then something which does not stand outside of the biological forces which shaped the nervous system but rather is an integral part of it. If the nervous system and the brain are capable of displaying a systematic logic in the solution of the problems of the organisation of its motor activities, we must ask if it might not be the case that deep within this motor logic lie also the origins of rational approaches to thought and problem solving with which we are ourselves familiar.

Certainly a logic of a highly sophisticated kind exists for the expression of motor movement. The essential step as far as those logical operations which characterise our own mental life are concerned probably consisted not of a disengagement of the logic system for motor movement for other functions, but the gaining of access to it for use for other purposes, a splitting off or rebuilding of the essential fabric of the machine in order that this may be put to the use of the decision systems of the brain. In other words, there is a divorce of the logic systems as tied to motor functions in order that logic can be expressed elsewhere and in other ways in the advanced organism.

Certainly a remarkable feature of the behaviour of many organisms low on the evolutionary scale is the very complexity of the logic systems necessary in the control of the systems of movement which they show. Yet at the same time each organism although in possession of a remarkable logic facility seem constrained to use this only in the control of motor movement and such organisms may show little in the way of learning or capability for the modification of behaviour in other respects. The wonderful precision, control, and sequencing of their movements is amazing but logic stops short there.

It is only in the higher reaches of the evolutionary scale that we see logic divorcing itself from the constraints of motor movement, or rather divorcing and duplicating itself and acting as a more pervasive feature of human intellectual function. Speech might be thought to be a particular example of this in man. In fact, however, speech provides an example of a system only partly divorced from a dependance on motor logic because it is the articulated sequence of motor movements in speech which gives it its grammar.

It has been argued that there is a grammar of behaviour. It is quite possible that this grammar of behaviour is itself derived from the primitive, and sometimes the not so primitive, arrangements for motor action in organisms occupying a lowly position on the phyletic scale.

Intelligence by no means consists only of the working out of some logical plan; nonetheless, that is a large part of it. It is tempting to speculate that in the complexities of the logic system for the control of motor movements in the programmes laid down for coordinated action and in the sophistication in setting the organisms along a particular course despite factors which may otherwise cause it to deviate from that course, lie the roots of intelligence as we know it today. Not a constrained biological intelligence but something permeating all aspects of human life.

Chapter IV

THE CEREBRAL CORTEX

Introduction

THE cortex is the deeply fissured mantle of
the brain which in man is the part which constitutes the largest
bulk. The cortex of man represents one of the major achievements of the process of evolution and in the human brain it is
distinguished by its relatively massive size. In fact, so much
tissue exists that to accommodate it within the skull the cortex
is folded like the bellows of a piano-accordian. The folds and
fissures are characteristic and it is their pattern which divides
the cortex into identifiable lobes. The cortex is the area responsible for higher mental activities, if there should be extensive
damage spreading over much of the cortex then there is a profound loss of the intellectual functions and the patient may be
seriously deficient in judgement, insight, and will. When we
discuss the actions of the cortex we are talking about the part
played in housing, fostering, and producing human actions be
it the capacity to think in a sensible and rational manner, the
ability to talk and act intelligently, the ability to compose a
piece of music or write a piece of poetry, or merely the ability
to derive pleasure from meditating and watching the sun go
down.

We encounter enormous complexity in the many intricate
actions performed so effortlessly in everyday life and it is clear
that few of the total number of the secrets of the cortex have, as
yet, been revealed. However, the most comprehensible approach to the cortex, and the one we propose to adopt here, is
to consider the functions of each of the lobes of the cortex in
turn and to describe something of the working of each part of
the brain although we are aware that in doing so, many general
features of how the brain integrates its actions could be over-
looked. In this way we can see that something of cortex func-

57

tions is slowly becoming clear.

Areas have been discovered which are concerned with receiving and analysing sensory information. What the eye sees and the ear hears as well as information from other senses is registered and implanted upon the brain.

The areas concerned are not merely passive way stations into the brain, rather they act as satellite computing systems at the outermost receiving end of the brain conducting their own analysis on the material which is received.

The information next gets passed into the fabric of the brain. It passes into the areas which organise coherent perceptions responsible for moulding and shaping the new data into the fabric of human experience and which we describe as the stuff of consciousness. Not only does the brain provide a running commentary on the world which we are aware of in the conscious sense, but it establishes equally well a running system for dealing with the world which we can sometimes remain totally oblivious of at the higher levels.

For example, we do not consciously experience the complex skills which we allow our brains to manifest when we ride a bicycle or drive a car. The woman who knits a pullover to an intricate complex design whilst at the same time watching television performs a series of complicated manoeuvres while barely thinking of them. The sum total of the workings of the brain are by no means those of which we are aware or those which we choose to designate as belonging to the higher reaches of the mind. The specialised contributions of the lobes of the brain are called upon as they are needed and the functions of each employed in the correct order and sequence. Finally, the brain organises sequences for coherent action which it translates into a useful end product of complex motor patterns.

The Occipital Lobes

The first part of the cortex we consider are the occipital areas which lie towards the back of the brain and are taken up with the process of vision. The importance of these areas to vision is demonstrated by the fact that if there should be severe damage at both sides of the brain then the person becomes blind because an essential part of the visual system has been destroyed. The eyes are preserved as normal but if essential parts of the brain or essential pathways acting to connect one part of the visual system to another within the brain are destroyed, then this can rob the patient of his sight. Not only is the visual system disconnected one part from the other by damage of this sort, but also some fundamental aspect of the working machinery of vision has been destroyed. The brain is no longer capable of functioning as before and this has a radical effect upon the patient's capacities.

There are various patterns of partial blindness from which it is possible to infer the nature and the position of the neurological damage. For example, the patient may go blind in only one eye or at only one side of vision, he may lose outer or inner vision, or his vision may be absent from some regular or irregular area of the visual field but present in the surrounding area.

One of the major symptoms of damage to the visual area of the brain is known as *scotoma*. The patient in this case can see with most of the area of his vision but there is an island in his visual field over which he is totally devoid of sight. The paradoxical aspect of this is that the patient himself may be unaware of the fact that he can see through only part of this eye. He sees no blackened area, no peculiar fuzziness or ring of visual artefact around the area, he sees nothing unusual in his vision. If he looks at a moving object, the movement does not stop when the object passes across this area of blindness. The clinician knows about this strange area of blindness because he conducts tests on the visual field. If he flashes a light to the blind area or shows to the blind area a picture of an object, then the patient fails to identify the object or the presence of a stimulus. Although there clearly is a region of vision which totally or in part fails to function, the question must remain as to how the patient remains largely in ignorance of this and how it is that the patient himself fails to see a lacuna or an area of distortion in his visual field.

One reason would appear to be that the eye itself acts as a

remote satellite computer, presenting a filled in or completed picture to the brain in spite of the fact that not all the elements are available to it. The eye in essence could present the brain with something like a map of the region it surveys, partly abstract and partly representative—a picture in which the irregularities have been smoothed out and in which the cardinal features have been etched in. Another factor is the compensatory capacity of the eye. The eye is in a continuous state of movement, fixating first upon one thing and then another.

It undertakes a series of scans across the visual environment. Despite the fact that there exists an area of blindness in the visual field the eye itself can ameliorate the effects of this by the pattern of scanning it adopts and by ensuring that through eye movements important parts of an object to be viewed fall on those regions of the eye which are possessed of sight. Finally, the brain itself is in command of remarkable powers of restitution and where damage exists to part of the brain the survival of activity is ensured and the protection of a particular function undertaken by the fact that an area can take over where a damaged area has failed. There seems to be every reason to suppose that this principle of *compensatory action* or *brain plasticity* operates with lesions of the visual areas as it does in other cases.

Although blindness of large areas of the visual fields or blindness in limited regions is characteristic following damage to the visual areas of the brain, there are additional disorders which do not produce blindness but result in disorders in the way patients are able to see the world. Damage to the areas adjacent to the main visual zones whose damage is associated with blindness do not in effect prevent the person from seeing but interfere more with the capacity to use the information flooding in through the sense of vision and to interpret such information in order to construct an adequate picture of the world.

For example, if the brain is stimulated electronically in these regions the subject experiences not bright spot flashes of light or visual flares passing in front of the eyes but complete fulfilled and assembled visual hallucinatory experiences. The patient in his mind's eye (or his brain's eye) sees something, some recognisable object or aspect of his experience complete and whole as though he is in fact witness to that actual thing. He may, for example, "see" a friend approaching him and beckoning him with his hand. This suggests that there are areas of the brain concerned partly with the store of the individual's life experience represented in visual form and with the capacity to build up meaningful interpretations of the world based on the nature of the visual information received.

When damage occurs to the secondary visual areas, the patient's approach to the visual world undergoes characteristic changes. The capacity for acute visual perception is diminished. The patient may be unable to combine individual features into complete forms. Perception regresses to a primitive searching and the patient, far from being able to grasp the significance of a picture or a scene in one glance, finds himself forced to scan each of the elements of the picture in turn in order to reconstruct, in the absence of immediate perceptual grasp, the nature of the object or the scene from its elements. In other words, there is a defect in the more advanced capacities of perception which can be described as the insightful synthesis of vision.

How this is achieved in normal unimpaired perception is still something of a mystery. Learning plays quite a large part in this. With familiarity and knowledge goes instant recognition with the consequence that continued inspection becomes less and less essential. With the growth of familiar knowledge goes hand in hand the development of the capacity for the immediate grasp. In other words, the perceptual system becomes a more efficient and highly tuned instrument as the years of opportunity for perceptual learning in childhood and in adolescence pass by. It is, however, this very facility for higher efficient recognition which is impaired by damage. The patient no longer grasps the overall picture but has to inspect each element painstakingly and with deliberation and only then can he identify and describe the pictorial material before him.

Luria describes how if the patient should be shown a picture of a pair of spectacles he at first follows the round contours. "There is a circle and another circle, a middle piece, it is a bicycle. No! Could it be a face? No! Spectacles perhaps!" The person with normal perception can detect from a glance that a certain outline is the shape of the human form. He does not have to follow the contour around, to count two legs, two arms, and a head before the shape can be identified as a man, whereas the patient with visual damage has to undertake this low-grade search. Thus the type of disorder involves the lack of capacity for high level integration of visual performance and because of this the patient can only acquire knowledge of the nature of the visual world by the process of search assembly, causing him to work essentially at reduced capacity. Some authors describe this disorder as a visual agnosia, i.e. a lack of ability to gain knowledge through vision. This, however, does not in reality describe the nature of the disorder which is perhaps best described as a loss of the capacity for *visual synthesis*.

The Temporal Lobes

The temporal lobes are situated to the side of the brain and correspond to a position on the head just above the ear. Because the temporal regions, although corresponding at each side of the brain are in fact physically separated by a distance, it seldom happens that patients have bilateral damage or at least damage occupying equivalent zones of the temporal regions at each side. One unusual case in which there was a bilateral damage is that described by Scoville and Milner in 1956. Here, the patient's memory was severely disordered. It might be thought that the surgeon had removed some part of the patient's memories just as he removed pieces of brain tissue with the aid of his knife.

The patient underwent bilateral temporal lobe surgery in 1953 at the age of twenty-seven years. An area of tissue of both lobes was removed. The purpose of surgery was to relieve severe epileptic seizures which could not be adequately controlled by medication. This patient showed no decrement in his level of general intelligence following surgery, in fact there was an improvement.

The outstanding change was the derangement of memory.

Temporal lobe damage disturbed memories as they were most recently laid down prior to surgery. This suggested that the surgery had acted not upon the earliest of memories but only selectively upon those stored most immediately before the insult to the brain took place. We could make an analogy to cargo vessels waiting to be loaded at the dock.

If there should be a strike of dockworkers then those vessels affected are not the ones loaded and already making for the open sea but those in the stages of the stowage of their cargo. The arrest is one which affects the stowage and initial loading but not the capacity to transfer cargo when once loaded. We may argue similarly in the case of the human brain that a certain amount of work has to be performed upon the stuff of memory to complete its stowage. An impression does not simply enter the brain for permanent storage as sound is recorded on a tape, but rather the brain works actively upon the memory. This is something not accomplished in an instant but over minutes, hours, perhaps days.

The evidence suggests that the earliest memories are not stored as unique units in the temporal lobes but elsewhere in the brain as well and they can be reconstructed by the participation of the other regions. The surgeon does not extirpate the patient's life experience at the time that he removes the tissue of the temporal lobes, what he does is to interfere with the capacity for storage in a permanent form. This may be because the communication mechanisms of the brain have been disrupted by the surgery, and restitution of communication networks is necessary before the memories can be reordered and the flow of memory into permanent storage in the brain can once more take place. The fact also that memories, although not available immediately after the surgery, subsequently become available suggests also that bilateral damage to the temporal lobes does not even remove from the brain that memory stuff awaiting consolidation. What it does is to shut down the executive office for the machinery of memory consolidation, the material, or at least a large part of the material, is still available but the instructions concerning its processing are lost.

The patient has a severe lasting memory deficit which was

reflected in all the events of his everyday life. He was unsure of his new address six years after the family moved. Also he was unable to learn where objects used frequently in his day to day existence were kept, objects such as the lawnmower. Because this patient was apparently unable to retain much memory of the events of his life he enjoyed completing the same jigsaws and reading the same magazines over and over again, presumably each experience of the magazine came to him fresh and there was a curious timelessness associated with the fact that memories which act as the marker posts of the passage of time were no longer registered by his brain. This dramatic syndrome is characteristic of many of the cases of bilateral temporal lobe damage so far studied.

It would be wrong, however, to state that this patient is totally deficient in all memory. The fact that he gets pleasure from reading magazines and is able to complete a jigsaw shows that some aspects of the memory process are accomplished and that some part of the mechanism is preserved. Indeed, without this fundamental capacity to retain knowledge, if only for a few seconds or minutes, all intellectual ability would totally disintegrate and the patient would be quite unable to register the nature of any of his experience. Because this capacity for short term registration is not impaired and because this represents something at the hub of the abilities of the brain, something which makes mental and intellectual life possible, the suggestion arises that this is an ability that should be more closely paired with the processes of perception and registration of information than with those aspects concerned with "memory" in the more conventional sense.

The patient in fact could remember small units and pieces of information. These he retained for a few seconds but if distracted, all was lost. Also it was rather curious that this patient had a capacity for learning which, although impaired in some aspects, was the equal of normal in others. This is strange because it might be thought that if he were severely deficient in memory then he also should not be able to learn fresh tasks because he would be unable to store the requisite information about the tasks.

Just as memory no longer marked out the passage of time for him, so its lack should impair his capacity to profit from past experience. He could not learn difficult maze tasks, but he could learn relatively easy tasks. He could learn to track objects on a task in which he was required to pursue a moving target, he could also sort cards and identify objects with increasing accuracy. One possibility is that learning is not a unitary pattern of activity. It is possible, therefore that brain damage could interfere with one type of learning and yet preserve others.

That the temporal lobes are implicated in the memory process is indicated further by the fact that when there is damage to the left hemisphere, the capacity for memory of words and verbal material is diminished. It seems probably that the basic memory defect is responsible for many of the disorders which surround and characterise damage.

An important part of the temporal lobes is given up to housing the auditory cortex. This is known as a projection area and this is the region where the fibres from the ear lead up to and play like a fountain upon the uppermost regions of the brain. The projections from both ears go to the temporal lobes at each side, the fibres from the opposite ear being the larger. Other areas close by are important in making messages understandable to the brain. If the brain is electrically stimulated in these regions the patient hears voices or musical tunes. These regions are probably the ones which make it possible for the person to disentangle the significance of complex chains of sound as occur in speech or in music.

With damage of the left temporal lobe the patient may lose this capacity for disentangling the sounds of speech, whereas at the opposite hemisphere the patient may lose the capacity for disentangling the elements of musical argument. Patients with damage to the left temporal lobe develop a number of characteristic disorders of language which depend on the site and the patterning of the damage. If the auditory areas are damaged, the patient may lose the ability to distinguish between the different sounds of speech. He is thus at a considerable disadvantage. It may be impossible for him to understand or comprehend the meaning of words. He may also have disorders in his own communication with others. It may be very difficult for him to produce the correct names for objects and he makes mistakes, particularly over closely related names. The patient himself may show disorders of speech, e.g. using a jumbled assortment of words which lack a coherent structure although it may be possible to derive something of their intended meaning. Finally, there may be an accompanying disorder of the ability to write. The running flow of writing transcribed from the current speech can show a severe deterioration.

In the case of lesions of the right hemisphere situated in the temporal lobe the picture is quite different. Here the disturbances of language are not much in evidence. Intelligence often shows a decline after the right temporal lobe damage. The decline is in the performance items of the intelligence test—assembling blocks and carrying out practical tests. The capacity for maze learning performance is impaired and this relates to failure in ability to orient and to "get around" in the world, generally called "spatial abilities's" but in fact representing far more than that rather flat description suggests. Much of the musical sense appears to be impaired in patients of this type. If two melodies are played to the patient at the same time, one to one ear and the other to the other, then the patient has impaired response to the melody entering the right hemisphere.

It is a striking fact that social psychologists—often so language oriented and preoccupied with studies of attitudes and values—have by and large not yet begun to study the effects upon the individual's social behaviour of damage to specified regions of the brain. That blame attaches to them for their neglect of this imporant area goes with out saying. What is the effect that damage to the brain has upon the individual's capacity to communicate and to carry on everyday social intercourse? How does brain damage effect the individual's interpersonal behaviour—sexual, aggressive, filial, parental, maternal, etc.? There are exceptions; it has been reported, for example, that a common disorder following removal of the temporal lobes is a low sex drive, although at the same time as the result of the brain damage there may be an increase in the number of patients showing sexual perversion. In summary, therefore, disorders which stem from damage to the temporal lobes are those concerned with the memory systems and those by which the patient receives communications and, in fact, himself communicates with the external world.

The Parietal Lobes

The parietal region is an area also towards the posterior region of the brain situated above the temporal and occipital lobes. The disorders which follow from damage to this region are not simply those of a direct disruption of the sensory processes. They play a part directly in intellectual activities and this is illustrated by the fact that when patients have parietal damage they lose the capacity to integrate their experiences into one coherent and overriding framework. The procedures which such patients adopt in their everyday lives are often fragmentary without any clear systematic programme of events which indicate that the patient has an adequate sense of how to achieve his purpose.

The patient in hospital, for example, who walks out into the corridor may be unable to find his way back to his own bed. If it should be asked of him that he carry out a task like making the bed then he may not be able to do so because he places first one blanket crosswise or makes some other very simple mistake. He fails to find his bearings on a map, he cannot distinguish the position of the hands of a clock to tell the time, and there is frequent confusion of his left with his right. In such patients there is a severe deficit in drawing possibly because the patient is unable to recognise what is to be drawn, or understand instructions as to what should be drawn but cannot orient himself properly within the context of the drawing. This difficulty extends to maps, diagrams, and other symbolic representations, as well as to letters and words thus interfering with writing capacity.

There are other aspects of life in which the patient fails. He may well understand the grammar of everyday speech but be unable to comprehend anything more elaborate. The capacity for tracing through a complex sentence, establishing the correct relationships, and conducting the necessary transformation of thought is considerably reduced. Like Hamlet when asked by Polonius, "What do you read my lord?" he replies, "Words, words, words."

Not only does the patient lose his way in the physical setting of the hospital and that of his immediate environment, but also he loses his way in the programme of his own actions with the consequence that the wrong actions are performed and inappropriate responses to the solution of the problem get made in spite of the fact that on occasion the patient may indeed have a good idea of the overall plan of action which he wishes to present. This difficulty of putting the appropriate programme of motor action into effect is known as *constructional apraxis*. This is more common with damage to the right hemisphere than to the left. There may be other effects, the patient may completely neglect the left half of the body. Strange interpretations of the body image may develop.

A loss of the ability to calculate is also found with damage to the parietal lobe. The basis for this disorder is not at present known. It may be that in the case of mathematical ability a search through the problem is involved similar to that of finding and orienting in a familiar or unfamiliar environment. The patient perhaps loses orientation to the problem and is no longer guided towards its solution by the signposts. Whatever the basic underlying cause, it is certainly the case that this disability is frequently typical of damage to this region.

The patients may have difficulty in recognising human faces and in gaining information from the human face necessary for the detailed signalling of moods and motives which the face provides in the communication between one person and another. It remains characteristic, however, that intellectual activity survives largely intact.

It was suggested at one time that these disorders following parietal lobe damage run together as a coherent entity. In our description of them we have implicitly suggested that they arise from a deep seated unitary function. It seems doubtful, however, that the unity of these symptoms is as ever present as perhaps has been suggested. Some or all may be present at any one time and it is perhaps best to regard the symptoms described not as an underlying syndrome but as a checklist for parietal damage.

The Frontal Lobes

It is clear that progress has been made in unravelling the functions of the frontal lobes, but it is equally clear that as yet the significance of this area must remain very much a mystery. At one time it was supposed that it formed a vast silent area which had no apparent function and the investigators were tempted to suggest that this enormous assemblage of brain cells was a sleeping, noncommunicating vestigial organ. This view was based on ignorance as much as anything else because a function had not at that time been fully attributed and the tendency was to assume that it did not have one. In fact, it seems unlikely that large tracts of the brain exist as areas devoid of function because the pressure of microminiaturisation is such as to impel each distant corner of the brain into useful service and to active life of some form or other.

The first suggestions about the nature of their functions came from the studies of animals when the frontal lobes had been experimentally removed in rats, cats, and monkeys. As we have already seen, one obvious approach to the study of what each part of the brain does is to remove that part in experimental animals and then to study the effect of this upon the animal's behaviour. By and large, such work has not fulfilled the original hopes for it here because dramatic interference with the processes of behaviour were not observed even after massive lesions to this area of the brain.

Some effects were observed, however, and among the first to be reported were that monkeys develop a disorder called the "delayed response deficit." This means that if the animal is prevented from carrying out a particular pattern of behaviour immediately, then it may subsequently fail to carry out that pattern of behaviour at all, or do so only at a low level of performance. In delayed response experiments, the animal is allowed to observe the experimenter place food under one of two cups but is restrained from actually removing the food by a barrier between it and the food cups. The memory for the deposition of the food is tested by removing the barrier at variable intervals of time.

The monkey with frontal damage can retrieve the food when only a short interval intervenes but is unable to do so over the longer interval. It seems likely that this result arises not because the animal's memory has been seriously disturbed (Weiskrantz showed that animals with this kind of surgery in fact can remember discriminations better than normal) but after removal of the frontal lobe the process of memory or what is stored in memory is disconnected from the system which takes information and translates it into patterns of behavior appropriate to the context. Since the time of the original animal work, which seemed to suggest that the animal with damaged frontal lobes had difficulty in utilising the memory processes, several investigations have been undertaken of brain-damaged man in which once again the frontal lobes were either severely damaged or had been removed by surgical procedures. Would the same difficulty observed after study of the behaviour of animals also be found present in brain-damaged men?

One patient with a massive frontal lobe lesion has been described by Luria. He was asked to lift his hand. The patient may begin to prepare the hand movement and his hand will perform slow movements, but these gradually become smaller and smaller in amplitude until they cease altogether. The patient may continue to repeat the command to himself showing that he remembers it yet at the same time utterly fail to carry out that command or to translate it into action. Another patient when asked to light a candle, struck a match correctly but instead of putting it to the candle, he picked up the candle and put the candle into his mouth as though it were a cigarette and started to smoke it. In all of these patients the verbal command remained in their memory, but it no longer controlled the initiating action and it lost its regulating influence.

The patient with damage to the frontal regions of the brain

also shows another disability which is of interest from a theoretical point of view, when such patients are fixed upon a certain course of action it may be difficult for them to change to a different one. Not only is there difficulty in making decisions about the future course of actions but also in switching when a decision has been made to change from one track to another. In other words, the patient loses flexibility and his capacity to adjust to environmental demands and the demands of his own internal physiology are diminished.

This propensity to follow one track to the disadvantage of overall performance is seen in experiments in which the subjects were required to sort cards into different piles according to the different criteria of colour, number, or shape, rather similar to sorting ordinary playing cards into number, suit, or colour. One group of patients sorting one way using a particular criterion, e.g. they had sorted all the red, blue, and green cards into different piles, now failed completely if they were required to sort them in a different way. Their tendency was to go on sorting them in the old way and to ignore the new.

Some investigators believe that this is a cardinal feature of the frontal lobe syndrome. It is precisely this inability to absorb the significance of the new or, at least once the die has been cast, the incapacity to respond in a fresh way as the consequence of the changes in the environment which is characteristic. Patients with frontal damage appear to have difficulty on several tasks which involve the assimilation of new information and the continuous correction of response in the light of it. That this is a question of the adaption to the new as it appears is evident. The disorder is clearly not one in which the patient is blind or unresponsive to information. The fact that it is possible to set the patient on an initial course of action shows this. However, when once set, the failure to respond to fresh information could result from the intensity of the action already taking place. The fact that there has been some major cerebral impairment which results in diminished attention to the task in hand has the consequence that the patient misses these signals which should set him on a fresh course. He is similar in some respects to the highly fatigued individual who keeps going when playing squash or tennis and although in command of physical stamina, loses the game because in keeping going he is unable to respond to the subtle new situations which develop in the game.

By and large, it is a matter of surprise that the deficits in intellectual function accompanying such a massive removal of vast areas of the brain are not more severe than those so far revealed. It can only be thought, however, that this signifies in no way that these areas are silent, diminished, or unresponsive in function, but rather that the methods so far employed, including the use of intelligence tests, have proved inadequate to reveal the functions which such areas may have, probably in the realm of the highest reaches of mental function. The areas most involved are those concerned with planning for the future and putting essentially practical courses of conduct into action. The ability, in other words, to size up the likely outcome of events, to forsee something of the probable course of future events, and to act accordingly, something one might describe as political skill in its widest sense.

Some of the most interesting observations concern the capacity of patients with frontal damage to conduct and carry out a visual search. There are many instances in everyday life where search is an important part of our normal behaviour. Not only do we search when we have lost a particular object which is available to us, but also we search on a variety of mundane tasks, for example, looking up a number in a telephone directory, selecting a newspaper from a stall, choosing groceries in a supermarket. It is an important fact about those patients with damage to the frontal areas that they are found to be deficient in this capacity for visual search. If the patient is shown a variety of objects displayed in front of him on a screen, he takes a long time to locate a particular target object even when that object is placed in the centre of his vision. One reason for this is that he shows a chaotic pattern of eye movements in looking at a picture, quite unlike the smooth fluid scanning of the main outlines of a picture so characteristic of normal vision.

This alone could be responsible for other deficits. The patient simply is not able to take in fresh information because of the chaotic scanning patterns which the pathology of the brain has given him. Just as the learner bicyclist preoccupied with maintaining his balance pursues a destructive course downhill not turning left or right and failing to negotiate obstacles in his path, so the patient pursues his course to ultimate disaster in performance because the capacity for the intake of information due to defective scanning patterns is impaired.

In patients with the most serious damage there can be a serious incapacity to express plans and wishes. The patient may express no wishes or desires and makes no requests. He may not respond directly to questions although on occasions he may join in conversations held with other people thus showing that the course of the conversation is being followed. It is not clear, however, in cases such as these that parts other than the frontal areas are not affected or that some degree of general disconnection has not been instituted by the depth and massive extent of the lesion rendering the brain a severely defective instrument.

In summary, it is clear that there are deficits to be observed following lesion of the frontal lobes. General intelligence as measured by intelligence tests is not generally affected to the extent which might have been predicted, but there are disorders relating to the capacity to put memory stored materials to work, disorders of plans of action, and disorders of motor programmes particularly those concerned with the uptake of information in the visual realms.

It seems in all probability that the frontal lobes have not yet yielded up their major secrets and that we may yet witness discoveries relating their functions to the highest activities that man can perform, those concerned with the creative and practically inventive aspects of human life. However, it should also be said that a view of this kind is largely an extrapolation based upon considerations of the evolution and the uniqueness of the human brain and we must await the verification through investigations before we accept it without question.

Cortical Localisation

The doctrine that particular psychological functions can be attributed to specific parts of the brain is known as cerebral localisation. Gall and Spurzheim, the founding fathers of phrenology, are generally regarded as the first proponents of this important view. Francis Gall was born in 1758; he studied medicine at Strasbourg and at Vienna where his discoveries were later announced. His doctrines were so popular that he was invited to become court physician to Emperor Francis I. The person who was eventually appointed to this position, Dr. Stifft, actually recommended by Gall when he himself declined, became extremely powerful and Stifft subsequently incited the clergy to prohibit Gall's lectures because of their materialistic tendency.

The idea of phrenology was that there are a finite number of powers of the mind. These are located in the brain and the degree of their development was to be assessed by the physical development of the brain in those regions of the power in question. Although phrenology is largely a discredited theory— because of the arbitrary division of the powers of the mind and the equally arbitrary assignation of these powers to different regions of the brain—nonetheless Gall is not forgotten. The importance of his work lies in the broader assumptions which extend beyond his particular theory and that is that those things we think of as psychological capacities and traits depend in all physical respects upon the brain and the machinery of our personalities and the control systems of our behaviour are located within the brain. Although that location may not be according to the exact scheme which Gall proposed, nonetheless much research has been inspired and guided by the broad aims which Gall set for his own investigations. In this chapter, we have had an opportunity to pursue something of this and to establish something of what is known about the cerebral localisation of function within the cortex.

However, a new and conflicting tendency was to be observed at work in the 1920s and 1930s which was fundamental in opposition to the views of cerebral localisation and the tradition established by the work of Gall. This can be described as equipotentiality which, as the word suggests, describes flexibility of brain function in the supposition that the activities of specific areas need not remain fixed and static. Although their actions may be imprinted with a characteristic stamp they can, according to the principle of equipotentiality, assume control over functions which were not previously allotted to them. The brain can in this way undertake a characteristic reordering of functions in the face of injury and physical damage which would not be possible according to the strict localisation point of view.

Lashley was a great pioneer of this view through his studies of the relationship of brain function to memory, learning, and intelligence. He began significant investigations of psychological functions in the laboratory rat. The study of brain function was undertaken by training the animal to perform a particular task, surgically removing a section of the brain, and afterwards reexamining the performance of the animal to establish that removal of that specific region had also erased the capacity for the performance of the task. The method Lashley employed, as we have seen, was to train a rat to run a maze to establish a memory of that maze in the animal's brain, surgically remove part of the brain, and then examine the performance of the animal in the maze once again to determine how much of the original memory of the maze remained.

In further studies, Lashley trained rats in a discrimination box in which they had to approach and pass through a lighted door in order to obtain food. Errors were punished by shock. When the rats had learned this discrimination, Lashley removed the visual cortex and retested the animals to study the problem of the relationship of traces of the visual cortex to the capacity of the animal to retain the habit of visual discrimination. Lashley reported that against all of his expectations there appeared to be no one specific site for memory storage in the rat's brain. A small lesion affected performance less than a large lesion but the locus of the lesion was not critical as he thought it would be. Thus a lesion placed in one area of the cortex had equivalent effects to a lesion of the same size placed elsewhere.

In respect to new learning also it was the case that the capacity of the rat to acquire knowledge of a maze was directly proportional to the size of the lesion in its cortex. If the lesion is large, the disturbance of new learning is considerable. As the result of these investigations, Lashley put forward his well known principle of the "mass action of the cortex" which states that it is the mass of tissue removed and not the site or specific locus that determines the deficit in learning. Lashley also suggested a law of equipotentiality which supposes that because the effect of a cortical lesion does not depend upon the specific site therefore one region of the cortex is equipotential in respect to another.

Several interpretations have been put upon the law of equipotentiality. It could be supposed, for example, that the cortex is equipotential for every function. This view is not supported by the fact that we know that there are specific areas for function, for example, visual or motor functions. It seems more likely that the cortex may be equipotential for learning and memory without necessarily being so in respect to other functions and that this more closely approaches Lashley's concept. In this context, it is the case that there are many examples both in animals and man where often no change in behaviour can be observed despite extensive surgical removal, provided a certain amount of tissue remains. Much of the subsequent work on the effects of cortical lesions has been inspired by the experiments reported by Lashley in his monograph *Brain Mechanisms and Intelligence*.

In the human brain, something of this principle of equipotentiality may be seen to apply. We have, for example, discussed the disorder of vision known as scotoma in which there is brain damage of small or large areas of the visual cortex that may nonetheless go completely unnoticed and undetected by the individual who suffers from it, and yet the presence of such damage can be revealed by the use of special techniques.

Teuber reports the famous cases of men who suffered missile wounds that had penetrated the skull and the brain. These studies were undertaken on men in the United States Navy, patients in New York, and a group in Boston, all with missile wounds to the brain. One case can be quoted of a previously normal young man whose visual brain was damaged during combat. This man had an island of blindness right in the very centre of his vision and yet he seemed to have scarcely any awareness of it. When he looked at a room he saw a room complete in every detail, there was no gap across the centre of his vision. If he looked at straight lines or patterned surfaces the lines or patterns did not stop across the area of his blindness, rather they were miraculously complete across his whole visual field. Yet there is no doubt that he was blind in these areas and this was revealed on tests in which he was asked to identify objects shown only to his blind area.

Although large areas of the visual area of the brain may be extensively damaged, vision nonetheless is preserved whole and intact in a remarkable way because the brain makes up for the deficit by filling the otherwise empty space with the pattern and substance of things around it. There may therefore be no conscious awareness of the damage which the nervous system has in fact sustained.

Another fact is that there seems to be equipotentiality of a remarkable degree in visual function because extensive damage may exist without severe consequence and damage to one area may have effects which are not all that different from damage to another area. For example, damage may affect the central regions of vision or the more peripheral areas and yet the patient still sees with remarkable clarity. However, much evidence from studies of human brain damage and surgical removal in higher mammals suggests that the brain may be far less equipotential than Lashley, as the original investigator, had supposed. The rat may not be the most suitable animal on which to test ideas of cortical localisation because its cortex is underdeveloped by comparison.

Also the possibility has to be entertained that maze running is an activity which employs numerous aspects of the animal's abilities. It is a composite and this may explain the results. If different abilities relating to different parts of the brain are used, all the animals when tested subsequently may show deficits but for essentially different reasons. It is also worth noting that other work has not entirely confirmed Lashley's findings. Rats reared in the usual type of laboratory living accommodation were equally impaired in maze running performance after lesions of the frontal and posterior cortex (excluding area 17) but rats reared in a free environment with much experience in a large mazelike living space were found to be more impaired after posterior than after frontal lesions.

Lashley thought that the explanation for his own results was that there was a widespread distribution of the engram for memory throughout the brain and perhaps there is. It is certainly the case that memories stored and represented at one hemisphere are passed over and stored also by the other hemisphere. Another interpretation can be put upon these most intriguing results, that is not only does a lesion remove an area of tissue which supports certain functions but the act of removal disconnects adjacent parts of the brain, as well as remote areas, from one another in this respect it leads to a much more general interference with function.

Brain tissue contains cell bodies as well as axons arranged into tracts leading from one part of the brain to another. The passage of impulses through these axons will be immediately arrested. The lesion, therefore, not only removes the functions and resident units of the brain but also creates widespread disconnection. The larger the lesion the greater the amount of overall disconnection and the more widespread it will be. A large lesion will produce a great deal of disconnection and this could explain why Lashley discovered an exponential relationship between the size of the lesion and the retardation of new learning.

The difference, for example, between a 50 percent and 60 percent lesion is very much greater than between lesions of 10 percent and 20 percent. The fact that it does not matter all that much where the lesion is in the rat brain again suggests that disconnection is at work and that the brain will be disconnected to the same degree by a lesion of the same size. The degree of disconnection is an important element in explaining the results. We may suspect that some degree of brain disconnection is a feature of almost all cases of surgical removal and it may be the degree of disconnection which has confounded attempts to establish the brain locus of particular functions in both the animal and the human brain.

Norman Geschwind pointed out the significance that the split-brain disconnection work can have in the interpretation of what happens when part of the brain is removed. He included his own work as well as the work of Sperry and Gazzaniga (described in the next chapter) as illustrating that a lesion can divorce one area of brain from another. The significance of the split-brain work from this point of view is that when the brain was split by cutting through the corpus callosum an area had been sectioned which contained only the axon fibres whose purpose was, as far as had been determined, to connect the two halves of the brain together. This band of fibres housed no cell bodies and so contained none of the working machinery of the brain, only the transmission lines across the brain. If such notable effects arise through the severance of communication fibres—disconnection as it was so aptly described—then the question arises as to how far the lesions in other parts of the brain also disconnect remaining areas of function one from the other.

The traditional view has been that the brain lesion removes an important area indispensable to function, i.e. part of the effective machinery of the brain. It is now clear, however, that a lesion wherever sited would also effectively dissociate some brain regions from others.

What we have to ask now is how far does a lesion in any part of the brain act to introduce a failure of communication of a specific or a general kind into the activities of a damaged or a disordered brain? In other words, how far does brain damage lead to a general breakdown in the communication system of the brain and how far and in what ways does surgical removal of cortex lead to a disconnection of some brain areas from others? Disconnection is something which may well occur between regions of functions within the hemisphere at the cortex as well as between regions at the surfaces of the cortex and the deep lying regions of the brain, and if part of the brain is surgically removed not only will the functioning elements of that tissue no longer be available but the lesion may also have disrupted overall relationships and, moreover, this may have been done in three dimensions.

There are yet other factors to consider in the effects which damage to the brain may have upon performance. Particularly important in this respect is the possibility that a lesion may not represent such an inert artefact as some investigators suppose. For example, removal of tissue even from a closely circumscribed area could set up a site which produces active interference with the remaining functions of the brain. It is known that it is possible to detect the imminent collapse and death of a brain cell before it actually dies because it gives rise to rapid but spasmodic electrical firing which is unlike its normal output. When brain tissue is severed, the death of cells around the lesion results. If a screen of electrical activity is set up this will be incorporated in the remaining ongoing functions of the brain and it will appear as interference. Furthermore, the effects of interference could register at parts of the brain quite distant from the site of the original lesion. An example of electrical disturbances transmitted to distant parts of the brain is that of focal epilepsy where an electrical disturbance at one site is transmitted through the fibre bundles to distant areas.

Another way in which a lesion at one site can interfere with areas distant from the lesion concerns those areas of the brain linked together to form a functional unit. The removal of part of the system may well destroy the function of the whole—just as placing a switch in the off position can prevent the operation of machinery at a distant source from the switch. Removal of one vital link can also destroy the function of a system in the brain, even if parts of the system are widely distributed throughout the brain. The possibility also exists that removal of brain tissue leaves other systems in a disrupted and inadequate state but one in which function is not suspended. Part of the system remains and it is this which continues to function, but it fails to function properly. As a consequence of such disjointed activity, false and disrupting information is fed to the rest of the brain just as ugly and untrue rumours can spread through a community to create social malaise. Again the source of this disruption is active and the effect of it is positive. This is not something caused merely by the absence of tissue and although it may operate only in the areas adjacent to the lesion it could equally well operate at more distant parts of the brain. It has always been a problem, therefore, to distinguish at which point a lesion has its effect in the chain of transmission of information. For example, a lesion could disturb the process by which the brain takes in information about the world. It could disturb the process of memory and learning, the decision processes, or the output system by which the brain translates commands into action. A lesion can disrupt this chain of events at any point.

It cannot be assumed that every aspect of a function from input to output has been universally affected but that interference has operated at only some part of the sequence. The significance of this is that there is an important and occasionally forgotten fact that output is essential and that it is possible even for competent investigators to refer to the lack of a system for intellectual functions, when what is lacking is an appropriate channel for output.

It is important, therefore, to note that a lesion has three or more possible effects: (1) It destroys a portion of functioning tissue. (2) It disconnects one area from another. (3) It disconnects input from output. We now have to consider this problem at a much more general level. We can state the general principle that all lesions wherever sited introduce some degree of disconnection into the brain. If a region of cortex is removed not only is the circuitry specific to that region destroyed but the passage of fibres passing through the linking across it to other regions is also interrupted. Brain tissue may be expected to take part in a transport of information; that is, it passes on information about the functions of one region to another. The removal of tissue produces an effective block to transmission across the shorter distances of the brain as well as transmission through long axon fibres to distant parts.

It might be argued that widespread disconnection of function as the result of a brain lesion should be followed by effects which are both specific and of a more general kind. The fact that there are specific effects is clearly illustrated in the disconnection syndromes. The fact that there are nonspecific effects, or at least effects which are not as yet traced to any one source, is demonstrated in much of the literature on brain lesions. There are frequent reports of disorders of volition, intelligence, foresight, and capacity to plan for the future, as well as disorders of will. Much of this is attributed to the effects of the pre-existing pathology but effects of this kind could also arise from a more general disconnection of the functioning units of the brain. The concept of disconnection is important in extending understanding of the effects produced by removal of tissue from the brain. It is not the intention, however, to suggest that disconnection is the only factor. Parts of the effective machinery of the cortex are obviously removed by brain lesions but disconnection is produced as well.

In summary, therefore, the question is posed as to how far disconnection is a common phenomenon of brain damage. It is believed that disconnection is a theoretical concept of considerable importance in the discussion of brain organisation and disorganisation, but also it is a concept which remains to be widely applied in the clinic as an interpretation of the effects of disorders of brain function. The question also arises as to the nature of disconnection in normal functioning. We are only at the beginning of an understanding of this but if the results of surgical disconnection have their parallel in normal brain, then we may expect that the way in which the brain acts is to connect and disconnect one region from another of its own accord. The problem now remains to establish the pattern by which this is worked out, particularly in respect to the distinction between conscious and unconsciousness brain functions.

There is little doubt that the cerebral cortex is the area of the brain of man where the most complex of the intellectual functions are performed. In this chapter we have attempted to specify something of those functions and the degree to which they are dependent upon the integrity of areas of the brain. Knowledge of the functions of the brain is more advanced in respect to some abilities than others, particularly in the cases of perception, memory, and speech and language. In other areas our knowledge is not advanced or as definite. In particular we are still a long way from understanding the learning systems and mechanisms of the brain. We are bereft of information as to how the nature of the damage to the brain in prescribed areas affects the individual's capacity for social conduct. We are still a long way from gaining insight about the part played by the respective areas of the brain in those aspects of human conduct which are most specifically human—the capacity to think creatively, the capacity to invent, to synthesize, and to integrate, the capacity to automate habitual behaviour and skills as necessary, in other words the life springs of intellectual functions. The problems are difficult to investigate but how important is their solution.

Chapter V

THE SPLIT-BRAIN
CONDITION IN MAN

Surgical Division of the Brain

IN RECENT years interest has centred on a thick band of fibres in the middle of the brain, known as the corpus callosum, which plays a part in bringing the two hemispheres of the brain together into a working relationship. It is estimated that the corpus callosum is composed of two million or so fibres which stretch across from one side of the brain to the other. Normally this band of fibres is embedded between the two cerebral hemispheres and is visible to inspection only by pulling the two cerebral hemispheres apart. When surgery is performed on this part of the brain the effect is to interrupt the communication which normally exists between one side of the brain and the other; this is known as disconnection.

First, it is important to remember that the effects of surgical division of the human brain are not all that dissimilar from the effects of surgical division of the brain in animals and that it was the work on split-brain animals which first demonstrated in a way that was unequivocal that the two halves of the brain can show a functional separation one from the other. Each side is capable of performing many tasks on its own, and each hemisphere can independently perceive, remember, and learn, and conduct most functions of the normal brain at some level of proficiency in its own right. For example, the monkey can be trained to discriminate between different wooden shapes using one hand. The normal animal trained with one hand shows mastery of a problem when using the other. In the split-brain animal although each hand could be trained to perform separately, the animal was unable to transfer what had been learnt from one hand to the opposite hand. The fact that monkeys were unable to transfer from one hand to the other was shown not only in the failure to solve the problem using one hand when trained on the other but also in the fact that animals trained with one hand demonstrated no awareness using the other that there is a problem to be solved.

Similar experiments have been conducted with cats in which one of two pedals, distinguished on the basis of touch, is pushed to get food reward. The animal is not allowed to see which pedal it is pressing. If the normal animal is first trained with one paw and then tested with the other, its score is 70 to 80 percent correct when using the untrained paw. In the split-brain animal, however, it is zero. Perceptual learning and memory thus seem to proceed quite independently in the two hemispheres in the split-brain animal. Split-brain studies show that each half of the brain has the capacity to solve problems in its own right when it receives the necessary information, that each has the independent capacity to perceive, to remember, and to learn, that each half of the brain is to a large degree separate in its functions from the other, and each half has little or no knowledge of the functions of the other.

With regard to the human brain, it is suggested that the picture is essentially similar; there are symptoms of the split-brain condition which characterise man and animals alike.

Split-Brain Man

Norman Geschwind and his colleague Edith Kaplan working in Boston, reported the first modern case of a patient in whom one half of the brain had become largely disconnected from the other. The patient was unable to identify a common object— for example, a hammer, a cup, or a packet of cigarettes—when it was placed in his left hand. In this classic case of cerebral disconnection the mechanisms for speech which occupied a position in the left hemisphere had become separated from the identification mechanisms of the left hand. In other words, the symptoms were those of the split-brain.

At much the same time surgery was carried out at the White Memorial Center, Los Angeles by Vogel and Bogen on a small number of patients who were treated with full split-brain surgery for the relief of servere and intractable epilepsy.

Sperry and Gazzaniga at the California Institute of Technology studied the patients of Vogel and Bogen and made note of the major symptoms that follow as the effect of splitting the human brain. There is an incapacity to cross-localize stimuli, there can be simultaneous functioning of each hemisphere, and each hemisphere has the independent capacity to perceive, to remember, and to learn. The functions of one hemisphere remain, except by indirect routes, unknown to the other, and right hemisphere activities are dissociated from the speech mechanisms of the left. These observations have been made on a small but unique group of patients.

The feature about the cerebral hemispheres relevant to the split-brain surgery is the fact that just as the eyes and ears are paired structures so there are two cerebral hemispheres, one at each side, which together form the cerebrum. The fibres which link the hemispheres together are called the commissures. The largest of these is the corpus callosum which is a crescent-shaped mass in the midregion of the brain. The corpus callosum is not the only commissure linking the two lateral halves of the brain, although it is certainly the major one.

In the human split-brain patients, the corpus callosum has been sectioned but so also have the other commissures, the hippocampal commissure and the anterior commissure. In some cases another structure, the mass intermedia, was sectioned. In other cases it was judged to be absent.

The corpus callosum reaches its most advanced form in the brain of man and it is in the human brain that transmission of information from one side to the other is most rapid. The fibres in the callosum connect up one point in one hemisphere with a corresponding point at a symmetrically opposite position in the other hemisphere. This principle of symmetrical connection applies to most areas of the cortex except the areas concerned directly with the reception of impulses from the sense organs—the eyes, the ears, and the areas of the body surfaces used for sensory exploration.

If we look in detail at the components of the brain, the cells responsible for brain activity, we find that not only are there millions upon millions of cells each with sensitivity and the power to sustain an electrical impulse, but that the cells interlink with one another to form the circuits of the brain. To facilitate interlinking, some cells develop cablelike extensions or axons which allow associations to occur with remote areas of the brain. The buildup of these communications is important to brain functions in general, but it is particularly important in respect to the cross-communication between the hemispheres because the corpus callosum is made up exclusively of fibres of this type. In primitive species there may be many thousands of fibres but in man there are as many as two million fibres and there seems little doubt that the development of this rapid conducting system between one side of the brain and the other represents a major advance in brain evolution.

The first split-brain case reported by Bogen and Vogel shows the hemisphere disconnection syndrome to a marked degree. To illustrate something of these features we include extracts of the following case from Bogen and Vogel (1962).

Report of a Case

Multiple head injuries at age thirty followed by blackout spells. Generalised convulsions beginning at age thirty-seven, progressively worsening. Cerebral commissurotomy at age forty-eight. No major convulsions for the first six months postoperatively.

Preoperative History

The patient was first seen at age forty-two at the White Memorial Hospital because of blackout spells for the preceding twelve years. His first episodes occurred several months after a parachute jump over Holland during a bombing raid in 1944. Incomplete opening of the parachute resulted in fractures of the leg and unconsciousness of unknown duration (approximately forty-eight hours). During subsequent internment in a prison camp he was rendered unconscious by a rifle butt blow to the left parietal region of the brain. Following his return

home he was employed as a payroll courier, but he was recur-
rently plagued by "lost time," i.e. periods of time for which he
could give no account. On one occasion he recalled driving
away from home one morning and arriving thirty miles away
that afternoon with no recollection of the intervening events.

In 1953 he had a particularly severe series of convulsions
lasting several days. Afterwards he had a profound loss of sensation on the left side of the body. This condition improved
rapidly but incompletely. When he was first examined the convulsions were recurring at a minimum of two or three a day.
They were occasionally preceded by an aura of dizziness described as a "Ferris wheel revolving." The onset of the seizures
was often related to emotional upsets. Facial grimaces and occasional utterances such as "Bail out, Jerry" were noted during
one period. Although speech and motion was slow and deliberate the patient's intelligence affect and insight were good.

Operation (6th February 1962)

The corpus callosum was exposed by blunt dissection with a
minimal amount of hemisphere retraction. The corpus callosum was sectioned. It was apparent that the blood supply to
the cortex was normally brisk in all distributions.

Postoperative Course

Following the operation there was a profound left hemi-
plegia but with markedly active reflexes present on the right.
Even when the patient could co-operate with requests (for example, protrusion of his tongue) he remained mute, unable to
feed himself, and without spontaneous movement for nearly a
week. Progressive recovery followed. Four months following
the operation the patient walked well and performed complicated bimanual tasks (for example, lighting a cigarette) without
obvious impairment.

In the second testing session, various points on the body were
stimulated. The patient was tapped at these points one to four
times according to a random schedule and was requested to

respond by tapping the corresponding number of times with his fingers on the palm of his hand. The difficulty in cross-localisation again became apparent. The patient could tap the correct number of times if the hand used and the place stimulated were located at the same side. If, however, the opposite hand was used, then the patient was unable to carry out this task. With regard to the sense of bodily position as well as pain and temperature sensibility, much the same picture emerged. The patient showed an inability to locate points of stimulation across the midline.

Another experiment is to present objects directly to the right or left hand for tactual recognition. The main cortical representation for the right hand is the left or major hemisphere, that for the left hand, the right or minor hemisphere. When blindfolded the subject can demonstrate the use of objects with both his right and left hand. Also a given object taken from the left hand can be retrieved from amongst other objects when the subject is using his left hand even though a time delay is interposed. However, it is important to use the same hand which held the object initially.

Follow-up Studies

This patient was followed up closely by Sperry and Gazzaniga using special tests of behavioural functions and we report the result of their findings on this and subsequent split-brain patients in the following section.

When during tests the patient was required to point with his right hand to a source of stimulation applied to the right side of the body, he was able to do so without any difficulty. Similarly, he could indicate the point at which he had been touched on the left side of the body with his left hand. When given a choice the patient almost invariably chose to use the left hand for stimuli on the left side of the body and the right hand for parts on the right side of the body. Parts on the head and face could be localised using either hand. Some of the later patients do, however, have some capacity to point to a source of stimulation on the body surface, whether or not it occurred on the same side as the hand. Patients also are to some extent able to overcome these difficulties of cross-integration of functions. One patient was reported to be performing cross-integrational tasks at well above the level of performance during the first year after surgery, and this patient at the time of reporting was continuing to show an improvement.

Further tests were employed in which the subject held both hands out of sight with the palm up and the fingers extended. He then pointed with his thumb to spots stimulated by the examiner on different segments of the finger and upper palm. The normal person can point to symmetrical spots on the opposite hand using the opposite thumb, but commissurotomy patients have difficulty in performing this task although some patients appear to be able to carry it out even after commissurotomy.

Sperry argues that we appear to be dealing with two distinct realms of inner experience—"one serving the left hand, foot and left half of the body about which the patients are unable to talk or to write and the other serving the right side of the body for which verbal communication is normal."

It is possible to flash visual information to the right or left hemisphere and if the subject looks straight in front of him at a spot of light, signals flashed to the left of his centre point project to his right hemisphere and signals flashed to the right project to the left hemisphere. In one experiment slides containing pictures of objects, letters, numbers, or other visual material were flashed to either the right or the left visual field at 0.1 seconds or less, which is too fast for the ordinary person to move the eyes towards the stimulus. The split-brain patients were shown a bright spot of light one-half inch in diameter flashed to either the right or the left visual field. The patient was required to point quickly to the spot where he had seen the light. A stimulus in the right visual field would be pointed at using the right hand or the subject could state where it had been. The stimulus in the left field could be pointed at only with the left hand the patient could not say where the light had appeared. When both hands were left free only the appropriate hand was used, the other remaining motionless.

In further experiments the subject was shown a figure flashed briefly on the screen. He was required to select a similar figure from a group of five cards placed in front of him. The right hand usually responded correctly to patterns flashed to the right visual field. The left hand responded similarly, although not as well, to patterns flashed to the left visual field. However, the performance of both hands was inferior when the information was flashed to the opposite half-field.

Observations of this kind suggest that the mechanisms of perceptual analysis are duplicated within each cerebral hemisphere. The patients have little difficulty in analysing the information coming from the world to either the right or the left. The difficulty they have is in relating the information of one hemisphere to that of the other. They can transfer information perfectly well from one modality to another within the single hemisphere but cannot transfer information in the same modality from one hemisphere to the other.

What is said about vision in this context may have to be modified to some extent in the light of the recent research which shows that some cross-integration between the visual fields is possible. The patient, for example, can identify the presence or absence of an object in the left visual field and say that he sees something there and he may well be able to state something of what the right hemisphere sees. Whether this represents an attempt by the brain to reorganise its functions in the face of the insult it has sustained or whether there are natural subcortical visual processes in normal man is a question which must await further analysis.

If pictures of objects are flashed into both right and left halves of the visual field and the subject is asked to describe what he sees, he reports everything that falls in the right visual half-field but he misses everything that falls in the left half-field. When a picture is presented in a randomised right-left schedule the subject insists that he saw nothing in the left half-field on that trial, or that all he saw was a flash of light. It is clear that the subjects are not blind in the left visual field but they are unable to talk about what they see. Thus we have the so-called major hemisphere of the brain that can talk and write and the so-called minor that cannot express itself in language. Sperry again suggests that these people have, in effect, not one inner visual world any longer like the rest of us but rather two separate and independent inner visual worlds—one for the right and one for the left half-field of vision—each in its separate hemisphere.

Trevarthen found in the monkeys he studied that it was possible to teach one task to one hemisphere and an opposing or conflicting task to the other.

Research has repeatedly shown that each hemisphere in the cat, monkey, and man can separately and independently learn discriminations of many kinds and that most problems trained in one hemisphere do not transfer to the other. When stimulus material was presented to the minor hemisphere under conditions in which its comprehension could be indicated by purely nonverbal responses, it became evident that the mute hemisphere was quite capable of perceptual understanding and of forming ideas of concepts that went well beyond a mere image of the stimulus. Not uncommonly these test performances involved some abstraction, generalisation, and mental association. This was demonstrated in tests that combined the presentation of visual pictures to the right hemisphere followed by the retrieval of a matching object with the left hand using touch. It is clear from this that the subjects can learn about the qualities of an object or a picture and use this to retrieve the object using the left hemisphere.

The capacity of each hemisphere for learning has been studied by Gazzaniga. The subject was required to learn a simple sequence of (1) or (0) flashed to the hemisphere. At the same time, the word "right" or "wrong" was also flashed. When both the task and the information as to whether the response was correct or not were flashed to the same hemisphere, the patient very rapidly learned the correct sequence but there was a complete failure when task information was projected to one hemisphere and knowledge of performance to the other. The task was insoluble to a person having no cortical connection between the task information in the one hemisphere and the critical correct/incorrect information in the other.

We have already seen that one noteworthy feature of the split-brain patient is the degree to which the speech processes are lateralised. The first patient, it will be recalled, could point with his right hand to an area of the right side of his body and with his left hand to the left side of his body. If, however, he was asked to state where he has been stimulated he informed the observer when stimulated on the right but generally failed to identify points of stimulation at the left. He may have suggested an answer but usually this stemmed from pure guesswork, and it was most often wrong. The patient was not uncomprehending but the right hemisphere lacked a connection to the speech mechanism. The first patient showed unilateral localisation of language and could not utter verbal descriptions of stimuli in the left visual field. When the stimuli were flashed one to the left and one to the right, he was able to describe the stimulus flashed to the right but denied any knowledge of the stimulus flashed to the left field. However, some note should be taken of the fact that in the original report it is stated that there was good reason to suspect damage to the right hemisphere coexisting with the split-brain surgery.

The second patient, after a few weeks, could not only point with either hand to touch stimuli on the opposite side of the body but also she could state verbally the position of the point where she had been touched. Subsequent patients have shown some restricted facility for writing and carrying out verbal commands with the left hand. The right hemisphere may be able to trigger a few simple words and is perhaps capable of singing and swearing, but for the large part it remains without access to speech.

A failure to be able to speak is not, of course, the same thing as an inability to understand or to comprehend. Recent studies have been undertaken of the understanding of the right hemisphere indicating comprehension through means other than speech. If short words, e.g. cup, orange, and pen, were flashed very rapidly to the right hemisphere, the subject was able to point with his left hand to the correct object. Similarly, if a picture of a ship was flashed to the left visual field, the subjects would pick up a card with ship written on it when using the left hand, although at the same time denying verbally that they had seen anything.

Another experiment was for the examiner to speak a test word and the patient to press a button when the correct matching word was flashed to the left visual field. The examiner also read a phrase, e.g. "Used to tell time" and the patient could select easily the correct word "clock" out of five words flashed to the left.

In another experiment, two pictures were projected on to the screen, one in the left half-field of vision and the other in the right, e.g. a picture of a pencil on the left and a knife on the right. The subject when asked says that he saw a knife, or if asked to write what he saw again he writes knife. However, if he reaches out with his left hand to select one object by touch, then he can. select the pencil when this picture is flashed to his left visual field. When the object has been retrieved correctly with the left hand and the patient is asked what it is, the right hemisphere tends to construct an incorrect answer which can cause the patient to wince when the right hemisphere hears the left hemisphere give the wrong answer.

In other tests a definition was first read out loud by the experimenter after which the subject explored a series of objects using the left hand without vision, ultimately selecting the correct object. By increasing the complexity of the definition it was possible to establish something of the comprehension of the minor hemisphere. The fact of comprehension of such complicated phrases as kitchen utensil for knife suggests that the right hemisphere has some capacity to perceive and to act upon spoken language, if not to speak it, and to express simple language through the control of the left hand. In an experiment in which a split-brain patient was given plastic letters to hold in the left hand it was found that the patient could arrange them properly to spell a word such as "can," "boy," or "pet." If the subject was asked which word he had spelled, in all cases he was unable to say.

In a more complicated experiment the subject was asked to hold an object in the left hand, e.g. a plastic key or a miniature book, and write the name of the object. In other words, he had to find the name and write that instead of copying what had been given to him. He achieved some success writing the first four letters of the name, but frequently he would stop and begin writing the wrong letters. This was interpreted as the speech hemisphere taking control leading to the production of the wrong name which could be spoken by the left hemisphere. The suggestion arises that although the right hemisphere has some capacity for recognition of short names, it may not be able to recognise and distinguish between verbs and that there is little in the way of syntactic ability. The exact amount of language capacity remains problematical. The fact that the hemisphere comprehends spoken commands indicates a high level of understanding, but with respect to visual performance the level appears to be reduced. There is some disagreement amongst the investigators as to the exact degree of sophistication which can be attained.

In this context it is worth noting that studies by Premack using an artificial language demonstrated a much higher degree of language ability in the chimp than had previously been reported and that Gazzaniga had used a similar artificial language with stroke patients who have been deprived of the capacity to speak by damage to the speech areas of the brain. The patients soon mastered the artificial language and of course the benefits of this in rehabilitation are considerable. This work suggests that the exercise of the logic of language is something not confined to the brain areas taken up with speech. The results taken together suggest that the right hemisphere does have some capacity to comprehend and understand language though perhaps to only a limited degree.

In addition to the left hemisphere specialisation for speech, which we interpret as unilateral control of speech output, there are other types of specialisation which were revealed by the split-brain studies. In one experiment a subject was given a task in which it was necessary to feel a wooden block with either the right or the left hand and to specify which of three blocks drawn on a card had been given. The right hemisphere showed itself to have complex qualities which could be readily visualised whereas the left succeeded on block sets requiring careful

analysis and failed on those which demanded a more
immediate grasp of spatial relationships.

The pattern of successes and failures in the performance of
the right hand hemisphere resembled more closely the perfor-

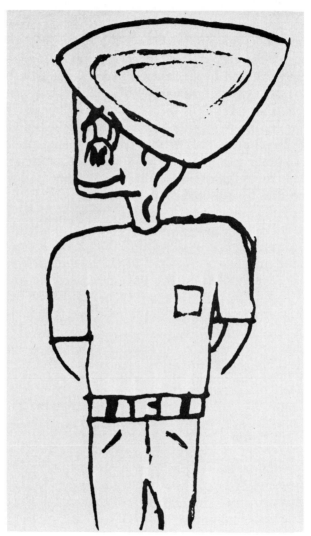

Figure 1. Self-portrait drawn by split-brain patient (with right hand).

mance of the right hemisphere of other subjects than that of its own left partner. This leads to the suggestion that the hemispheres employ different strategies and deal differently with in-

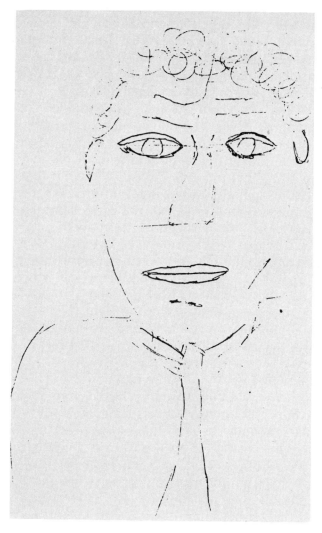

Figure 2. Portrait of the author drawn by split-brain patient (with right hand).

formation reaching them from the external world. The right with its grasps of spatial relationships apprehends events in a Gestalt fashion, whereas the left carries out a sequential analytic procedure. When sensory information is flashed to the right hemisphere good performance is achieved by the left hand on nonverbal tasks. Fine individual finger movements and mimicking of hand, thumb, and finger postures is readily demonstrated; objects like cigarettes, keys, and glasses are all manipulated with appropriate dexterity.

A surprising fact about left hand functions was revealed in the first patient. This person had never used his left hand previously for drawing and yet after the surgery he retained the capacity for drawing spatial structures with his left hand but not when using his right. A three-dimensional drawing of a cube and other spatial patterns were correctly reproduced when the left hand was employed, but the right hand showed very poor performance. Constructional tasks such as repeating a pattern of coloured blocks were also performed poorly by the right but well by the left. The left hand did consistently well and the spatial superiority of this hand was observed in a number of other patients, although some patients tended to recover a capacity to draw using the right hand.

The likelihood has to be entertained, therefore, that the right hemisphere has the greater facility for spatial functions. However, it may be unwise to describe the right as a hemisphere which uniquely fulfils the spatial functions for the reason that copying diagrams and assembling blocks into patterns may represent only a small part of what are generally regarded as the spatial functions. It is an interesting point that the right hemisphere has now been shown to have a consistent superiority in the performance of different types of geometry.

We have described the most important symptoms of the split-brain condition. The principle fact is that one hemisphere is unable to inform the other of its activities and that there is a failure to transmit information across the brain. Both hemispheres have the facility to remember and to acquire new learning; the right is specialised for spatial function and the left for speech, but both comprehend, understand, and possess the capacity for rational thought.

As we have seen then, the split-brain work of various kinds demonstrates very clearly that the capacity for perception is something which resides in each hemisphere. The cerebral hemispheres may not be equal in their contribution to the processes of visual perception and each may have a particular individual contribution to make and yet there is strong evidence that each plays an active part and that the split-brain person has two high-level hemispheric perceptual systems each working separately, independently, and in ignorance of the functions of the other.

The Intact Brain

We come now to consider the capacity of the normal intact brain. In the intact brain the corpus callosum forms a bridge between one side and the other which enables contact to be maintained and information to be passed across. The presence of the corpus callosum preserved intact and functioning fully need not detract from the capacity of each side to act as a perceptual system. The corpus callosum need no more rob any one hemisphere of its visual function than the facility of travel by international airline robs the states which it interconnects of national sovereignty. In other words, the split-brain cases illustrate in a dramatic way something that may well be true about the processes of perception whether the two systems are connected up or not, and that is that the higher functions of perception assume a bilateral form by which some of the work is completed in one hemisphere and some in the other.

We cannot accept the view that the brain acts as a single channel in its analysis of information or as a single channel where several stages of analysis occur in sequence. Further evidence, reminiscent of the split-brain, which strongly suggests a dual perceptual capacity at each side of the brain in the normal individual was obtained in our own work. We flashed half of one perceptual figure to one half of the brain at the same time as the other half of the figure was flashed to the other hemisphere. We found that people could match the two halves of the

figure more successfully when each half of the brain was pro-
ductively employed and in receipt of its own information. Even
in the case of everyday perception, the brain uses its bilateral
perceptual capacities to be a more effective mechanism.

In all likelihood, both hemispheres are engaged actively in
the task of making sense of the rush of information which
enters through the perceptual systems. The very fact that the
sensory pathways themselves are distributed to divide up information between the two halves of the brain lends validity to
this view. One simple model of the hemisphere function in
perception is to suppose that they work like the telescopes used
to investigate the three-dimensional structures of the Crab
Nebula. It is possible to reconstruct a three-dimensional model
of a supernova despite the fact that it exists far out in space.
The object is photographed, scanned for radioactivity, and observed through two different telescopes placed some distance
apart on the earth's surface. The data received by one is in large
measure the same as that received by the other, but because the
two telescopes view the object from different standpoints the
information they receive will not be exactly same but subtly
different. Telescope A views slightly to one side of the object,
telescope B slightly to the other side. When the input from the
two telescopes is compared using a computer, a three-
dimensional model of a very distant star can be constructed
here on earth.

The brain likewise creates three-dimensional images of the
world. The bilateral brain, we suggest, plays an immediate and
direct part in the analysis and reconstruction of the world in
three-dimensional terms. We cannot ignore the opportunity
which the brain has for an elaborate three-dimensional system
in the use of its two visual receivers. The normal single unified
picture which the individual constructs of the world can break
down into experiences of double or even fractional vision. The
apparent unity of conscious experience of vision should not be
taken as evidence that the process of vision is accomplished in
one sweep or that component working stations are not involved, anymore than the unity of the picture viewed on our
television screens is evidence that this operation is not com-

posed of a myriad of separate processes.

When a stimulus appears to one side of vision its registration exists in the brain only at one hemisphere and that object can therefore be immediately labelled as coming from that side. Objects at the periphery of lateral vision are represented at one hemisphere but objects occupying a space at the centre of vision stimulate both hemispheres. Comparison of hemisphere input pinpoints the exact position of the object and contributes to the essential mapmaking function of the brain.

If we consider a stimulus moving from one side of vision and progressing over to the other, like a star moving across the sky, the stimulus of that object registers at first only at, for example, the right hemisphere. As it moves more towards the centre, the other hemisphere picks up the stimulus and the object now begins to register on it. As the object moves across so the image registers more and more strongly on this second hemisphere until as the stimulus reaches the centre of vision both hemispheres are actively stimulated by it (possibly accounting for the power of central over peripheral vision). When the stimulus moves away to the right then initial representation at the right hemisphere gradually diminishes leaving direct stimulation to be effective at the left hemisphere alone. Thus there are very obvious clues about movement which can be gathered by comparison of the input to the hemispheres. The similarities and the differences in the pattern of visual impulse registered at each side of the brain could be responsible for the ordering of space in a three-dimensional way.

It is clear, however, that this is not the end of the story. Not only could the visual arrangements so far discussed play a major part in the ordering of static three-dimensional space, but we may also suspect they have a role in registering something of the flexible dynamic qualities of the changing environment. Does the fact that the changing images, which transform themselves over time, occupy a different balance in their representation between the visual systems at each side somehow endow the individual with an enhanced capacity to detect visual movement? An image near to the person which is seen to move will glide rapidly across the maplike projections of the brain. Near objects produce a rapidly gliding and changing configuration across the two halves of the brain, which is not paralleled by that of distant objects, and it would be surprising if this information were not fed into the melting pot of visual perception, but in conjunction with other sources to provide the reconstruction of distance, depth, and movement. The truly collaborative efforts of the two halves of the brain are probably seen in the richness and depth which their interaction gives to some of the more complex processes of visual location.

In confirmation of the interpretations made here we quote an observation of Zaidel and Sperry in which stereoscopic vision was tested by means of random dot patterns presented separately to each visual field which when combined produced a normal image. Patients in whom one of the cerebral hemispheres had been removed (hemispherectomy) failed to perceive depth on all of these tests, and whilst the commissurotomy patients did not fail on black and white dot stereograms (possibly because of subcortical transfer) they did fail for the most part on coloured stereograms which was interpreted as a disturbance of balance between ipsilateral and contralateral visual systems operating near the vertical midline.

Recent Developments

Commissurotomy is something which does not leave the individual without defects of various kinds. In particular, defects of memory have been noted which seem to relate directly to the loss of the corpus callosum. The patients have been, for example, notably unable to remember appointments or telephone messages. They fail to remember where they put things and they may forget how to get back to a parked car. Memory tests administered several years after surgery show that the patients are markedly deficient compared with members of the general population, and this is so whether the whole commissure or whether only the anterior two-thirds has been sectioned.

Neither hemisphere is devoid of the capacity for memory and it is all the more interesting in view of this that the defect should have been noted. In addition, perseverance on tasks that are mentally taxing remains low and there is a general impression that the patient's average mental potential is affected by the commissurotomy.

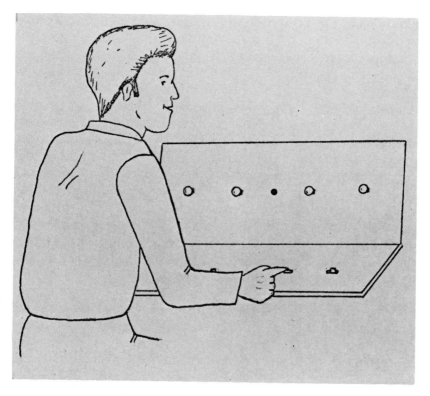

Figure 3. Patient carrying out vigilance task. From Stuart Dimond, *Brain, 99,* 1976. Courtesy of Oxford University Press.

These are not only the only deficiencies which the split-brain patients have been described as possessing. One suggestion is that the split-brain patient is deficient in the production of consciousness and thus the corpus callosum appears to be implicated as at least part of the system by which consciousness is maintained. It seems unlikely in view of the fact that the corpus callosum does not contain cell bodies which would involve it in the processes of decision and analysis, that it is the centre of the consciousness processes of the brain, rather it would seem with its extended system at each side of the brain to act as the monitor of the processes of consciousness.

Sperry describes much of the evidence which is relevant to this question. For example, Sperry reported that one gets the general impression from working with these patients over long periods that their overall mental potential is affected by the commissurotomy. Perseverence in tasks that are mentally taxing remains low in most of the patients, as does the ability to grasp broad, long-term or distant implications of situations.

It is also a fact that a loss of what might be called mental grasp is illustrated in other areas of the patients' performances. They score, for example, consistently low on the digit symbol and arithmetic subtests of the Weschler Adult Intelligence Scale. Also in other tests the patients have difficulty in keeping track of more than three patterns perceived sequentially by touch. This suggests a loss of sustained attention. Something of the loss of this capacity is seen in tests of motor function, where the patient performing a task competently over a period of time may suddenly cease work, stop, look up, and say, "How do I continue?" despite the fact that his performance has been adequate to that point and the nature of current performance demanded of him is no different from that demanded previously.

That there is a loss of the capacity to sustain performance is evident from these remarks, whether this loss comes under the category of a deficiency of the production of consciousness is something for debate. The evidence, however, seems to point in that direction. In studies of the vigilance capacity of split-brain patients the present author found that the split-brain patients showed long gaps where they existed apparently in an inert state and remained so often for a considerable period of time, failing totally to detect the signals that were flashed during these times. The capacity to remain in touch with the world is obviously something directly related to the study of consciousness itself, and during those times over which the individual fails to show the customary link to the processes of the environment he may be described as lacking in some aspect of consciousness. Consciousness is a strange animal and it may be easier to say when it is or is not present than to say what it is. In some measure, consciousness is a discontinuous thing, even in the normal individual it may be made up of functioning units interspersed with gaps. The gaps displayed by the commissurotomy patients, however, go well beyond anything seen in the conscious functions of ordinary man and for this reason they could be described as the black holes of consciousness.

They represent a puzzling phenomenon of brain disconnec-

Figure 4. Drawings on top produced by a split-brain patient before surgery. Drawings on bottom produced by a split-brain patient after surgery (drawing on the right done with the right hand, drawing on the left done with the left hand). From Dimond et al., *Brain, 100*, 1977. Courtesy of Oxford University Press.

tion and demonstrate a surprising way in which the total commissurotomy patient is lacking in the amount of consciousness of the ordinary man. Time out from an active relationship with the world can have debilitating effects upon performance but more than this, there is a degrading of some part at least of the conscious process by which the individual maintains a fluent and sensitive relationship with the world. The presence of large gaps in the mental activity of the split-brain patient suggests that consciousness is like an old stocking, good in parts but full of holes.

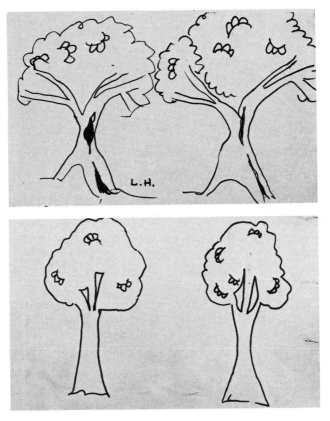

Figure 5. Drawings on top made by a split-brain patient before surgery. Drawings on bottom made by split-brain patient after surgery. Note the impoverishment of design. (Figures on the right drawn with the right hand, figures on the left drawn with the left hand.) From Dimond et al., *Brain, 100,* 1977. Courtesy of Oxford University Press.

Split-brain man, due to the lack of the commissural fibres, shows a failure in the mechanisms of consciousness. Sperry (1974) has suggested that the mechanisms of consciousness, i.e. the phenomenon of subjective awareness, are in principle restricted and capable of being localised within the human brain. He regards the interhemispheric commissures and their cortical associations as continuing to offer promise in the search for a direct correlation between neural structures and the complex states of subjective experience. It has now become clear that in these studies of the defects of consciousness in split-brain man, we have discovered a cortical system for consciousness which lies towards the back of the brain and which straddles the brain running between the two hemispheres using the callosum as an interconnecting pathway. The discovery of this system represents an important advance in our knowledge of how the processes of consciousness are conducted by the human brain.

Chapter VI

THE INFANT BRAIN

Ideas of Development

FROM time to time something happens to remind us that that which we may think to be permanent, in fact, undergoes a process of change. The crocus sprouts, blooms, flowers, and dies, the clouds swirl across the sky their natural movement speeded by the photography of lapsed time, the photograph album shows the growth of our children whilst we the parents become older and begin to sag at the knees. Change is apparent in all these but change is also evident in the range and cycle of human abilities. The abilities we have, arrived not in a single stroke but as the result of a barely perceptible process of growth and development, a subtle enhancement and a gradual movement from one stage of elevation to the next. They were constructed in the brain by sustained building one dependent upon the other. As Mark Twain said, "Soap and education are not as sudden as a massacre, but they are more deadly in the long run." As Hobbes expressed it, "The child is father to the man." and although the last thing that children themselves would think of their behaviour is that it is a preparation for what they are to become, nevertheless many things, even the patterns which they show by playing one with the other, can act as a preparation. Freud pointed out that there is a process of development for sexual behaviour through different stages in early infancy and childhood, and equally so for the whole range of abilities. The pattern laid down in childhood is often crucial to the subsequent development of behaviour and the way that this is expressed in adulthood and in later life.

In order to understand the individual we have to understand the history of that individual. To understand how the brain acts now it is essential to know something of influences by which that brain has been affected in the past. The study of the interaction between the brain, the influences brought to bear upon it, and the behaviour to which this leads is of critical importance because it sets the pattern and crystalizes the course which future events will take. If the brain fails to develop properly during early infancy or it sustains an injury at this time, the consequences which follow are such that the person may have to live with them for the rest of his life. The brain is able to compensate for damage but there are limits to the extent to which it is able to do so; severe damage may leave a permanent residual.

It is important, therefore, to know about the workings of the brain in the very young, not only because the full flowering of abilities stems from the action of the brain at this time but also because of the practical importance which such knowledge will have. If the brain fails for any reason to develop along proper channels then some disorders of behaviour may result which manifest at that time in the child's life, but the disorder can also affect the subsequent schedule of all later development.

Development of the Brain

The march forward of abilities from childhood to adulthood can be viewed against the biological background of the physical development of the brain. This follows a remarkably similar course from one person to another. It is therefore possible to specify the programme for development with some accuracy although, within limits, it is accelerated in some individuals and delayed in others. Development proceeds along a chain of events in which each unit of the chain occupies its own determined place and the relationships it holds with the earlier and later links of the chain is something fixed and inviolable.

The differentiation of the nervous system takes a complicated predetermined pathway. The nervous system appears as a plate of tissue in the developing embryo at the age of eighteen days. During the next seven days the walls of this embryonic plate grow upwards and over forming a tube which seals itself and then gradually sinks from a position on the outside of the embryo to one deep below the skin.

The neural tube is the basic structure from which the brain and the spinal cord develop. At the head end, the tube begins to swell and three enlargements appear which later become the forebrain, the midbrain, and the hindbrain. The rest of the neural tube takes up the sequential characteristic and steadily emerges as the spinal cord. The architecture of the nervous system is already laid down.

Even before the third month of foetal development the brain itself is beginning to change and show the features which make it resemble the adult. The topmost part is differentiated from the rest to form the cerebral hemispheres. These appear as bulges on each side of the tube. The area later to become the thalamic region separates. The brain grows two stalks which proceed towards the exterior surface to develop in due course into the retinas of the eye. Further back outgrowths appear which are the beginning of the cerebellum, a feature foreshadowing the organisation of this part as it is to appear in the adult brain.

During the next few months the cerebral hemispheres swell and expand as the result of growth of their tissue. The brain has to fold the tissue in concertina like patterns to accommodate it within the cranium. By the end of the fifth month the convolutions or folds which mark the surface of the cerebral hemispheres are clearly visible but the organism itself may still be very small; it is remarkable that it proceeds so far and yet the body is so tiny. The embryo is clearly recognisable as a miniature man after only a few months. From there on the main organs of the brain expand and increase in size and most of the features of the brain are now present.

One curious fact about the brain is that once formed very little significant increase in the number of neurons occur. A few may be formed during the first few months of life but essentially the neurons with which we are born are the only ones that we are likely to get. What we do is played out on the basic instrument with which we have been endowed at birth.

The brain of a baby at birth weighs 350 grams, that of the adult human 1,300 to 1,500 grams and 95 percent of the adult weight has been obtained by the time the child reaches the age of ten. The question arises therefore as to what is responsible for this increase. There are at least two answers: (1) The population of neurons although finite may themselves increase in weight during the process of maturation. The pathways of the brain become more complex during development. Nerve cells create connections one with the other and grow many links. The axons themselves become larger and many myelinated when they were not so before, i.e. they become surrounded by a fatty sheath. (2) There is an upward spurt in the growth of glial cells, cells in between the neurons are not restricted in their numbers as are axons. These cells form an important mass of tissue which increases rapidly during the first eighteen months of life.

Beginnings of Function

At the time of Plato the idea was current that the foetus was a living creature which had independent movement and which fed within the body cavities of the mother. The idea that the embryo had a soul, the theological aspect of embryology, was expressed in the writings of Aristotle. The embryo, however, possessed not one soul it was said but several souls each entering in one after the other. The first soul was of a vegetative kind, somewhat similar to that possessed by other living forms particularly plant life. A sensitive soul then developed, the soul typical of the animal, the soul by virtue of which the animal is an animal. Finally, the rational soul enters and the embryo takes on human form. The embryo seems to live first the life of a plant, then the souls are formed which change the creature in an animal direction and subsequently into a human form. The writings of Aristotle were an important influence on the early church fathers. Saint Augustine held, for example, that the soul entered the body in the second month of gestation.

The foundation of sex discrimination was laid in these early doctrines, canon law for a time recognised the fortieth day for males and eightieth day for females as the movement of animation. The views of Thomas Aquinas many centuries later did not differ substantially from those of Aristotle. He held that the foetus at first had a vegetative soul which perished at the moment the embryo came to be in possession of its sensitive soul which again died, replaced in turn by its rational soul provided directly from God. Other teachers held that the soul was infused directly into the individual and a distinction need not be made as to whether the foetus was formed or unformed.

It is not our purpose to dwell on the question of the time at which the soul does or does not enter the body. We are concerned only with the part the brain plays in regulating behaviour and the way in which the unfolding of the activities of the brain allows the individual to indulge progressively in behaviour which is characterised by an increasing range and sophistication. There is some development of behaviour which occurs during the latter stages of embryonic life. When the foetus is removed while still alive from the mother's body after the termination of pregnancy through maternal disease, movements are to be observed caused by the beating of the heart. This can occur as early as the third week after conception, although the embryo is minute and even the limb buds may not yet be formed.

The first true movements of the limbs occur as early as six weeks of age. Independent movements of arms and legs are noted at this time. Wormlike movements of the arms, legs, and trunk have been noted at ten weeks. An energetic protective movement pattern may also be observed in which there is strong action of the arms and hands coupled with the opening and closing of the mouth.

As the embryo develops, more and more patterns of behaviour appear and the range and flexibility increases. The embryo gradually becomes sensitive. At two months of age, stroking and tapping the skin produces slow contractions of all the muscles of the limbs. Response to touch occurs over the body surface but the back of the head remains insensitive to the age of thirteen weeks, gradually this area becomes sensitive also.

The evidence which exists suggests that the movement patterns in early embryonic life are controlled by the lower and presumably more primitive parts of the brain. Doubt has been expressed as to whether the cortex, ostensibly the higher part of the human brain, comes into play as an organ capable of controlling behaviour until quite an advanced stage of early infancy has been reached.

In an early Italian investigation which would probably not be contemplated today, the skull was removed of a prematurely born foetus just as death seemed imminent and the brain was stimulated electronically. It was found that if the lower parts of the brain were stimulated this led to specific effects such as an increase in breathing rate and in shoulder, arm, and finger movements. All these aspects of behaviour are apparently at this time under the control of the lower brain areas. When the topmost part of the brain, the cortex, was stimulated there was a completely negative result. The developing embryo may exist in a state strongly resembling sleep in which the upper parts of the brain are largely shut down, or alternatively the higher reaches of the brain do not yet show a flowering of their abilities which presumably occurs in the first years of infancy. Recordings of the electrical activity of the brain of babies born before coming fully to term also suggests that the brain follows a specific pattern of maturation and that in these infants the pattern of electrical activity is very primitive indeed. It seems that the cortex is not capable of sustaining action at anything like the level, say, of that shown by a two or three-year-old child. There is a definite maturation of the brain which proceeds along a chronological line whether the baby is born or not.

Towards the latter stages of pregnancy the unborn baby enters an active stage with frequent movements followed by relatively quiet periods. The baby, even before it is born, is highly active and although we do not as yet know very much about the brain functions of infants before they are born what we do know suggests that the brain is likewise active in some of its parts long before birth. It emits primitive electrical activity and already exercises some control over behaviour.

Some evidence suggests that the infant before birth is capable of learning. The unborn foetus is responsive to sounds. If a

sound of sufficient intensity and suddenness, e.g. a clapper
board or the ringing of a bell, is made close to it, then it shows
movement which can be detected through the mother's body
wall by sensitive instruments placed upon her stomach. If a
vibrator is placed upon the abdomen and is activated just before the sound stimulates the foetus, then after training, the
response made originally to the sound alone moves forward in
time and occurs to the action of the vibrator. It was suggested
that a connection is formed in the brain. The signal preceding
the noise acts as a warning of its imminence and the brain of
the developing infant is capable of making the association to
show learning, although still in a relatively underdeveloped

Figure 6. Child's drawing, age four.

state. The experiences of the world are beginning to penetrate the nervous system of the young organism and like the prince who wakes the sleeping princess with a kiss after one hundred years of sleep, so experiences act upon the brain to open up pathways that have so far remained dormant. The brain begins to function in preparation for life after birth through the use of its nervous system.

The brain of the baby now undergoes a period of expansion during which not only does the physical size of the brain increase but the range and complexity of the abilities that the brain controls is considerably enhanced. At this time the child is learning to use its abilities, to make sense of the information which enters its brain, and to manipulate its environment. This can be seen as the constructive ordering of experience, a progressively greater interaction with the world. At a time when the infant is particularly responsive to the environment and in the human brain learning and storage of information is carried out on a monumental scale, it would be surprising if somehow this were not reflected by parallel changes in the workings and structure of the brain.

Wilder Penfield expressed the idea that at first the cortex is uncommitted, i.e. patterns of action are not at first laid down. It is through use that the structuring of the cortex comes to be established. According to Penfield's view, the cortex whilst not infinitely plastic is at least markedly plastic during the first few years of the individual's life. The cortex is capable of taking up those functions which get superimposed upon it. At the early stage of infant life the capacity for this is almost unbounded but the cortex is never in later life able to sustain the imprint of use to quite the same degree. The very process of learning involves commitment and the laying down of learned engrams within the brain. With the capacity for learning goes also a narrowing of the potentiality of the brain for fresh learning. The very act of storing the massive supply of knowledge about the world passed through in childhood, the very act of ordering the brain along certain channels, the act of building an extensive repertoire of skills means that with commitment the sphere of action for acquiring fresh knowledge and for building in fresh skills is reduced—not entirely eliminated but reduced by a considerable margin. This is apparent for example in the case of language learning where some of the difficulty of learning a second language later in life may be attributed to the fact that the first language has already been learned. Frank Muir pointed out that when Rome conquered most of the known world it set up schools in all its newly acquired territories where the children of conquered nations had to learn Latin, an unenviable task which gave the conquerors a distinct advantage and in the words of Heine, "The Romans would never have had time to conquer the world if they had been obliged to learn Latin first of all."

The situation is rather similar to the student at school who may well be proficient in a range of subjects but he has to specialize in some and to drop others. As his specialisation increases so he becomes more and more adept in those subjects, but his knowledge and expertise in other subjects tends to fall away.

Injury to the Brain

In this connection one of the major features which indicates the sensitivity for learning and at the same time also acts to distinguish the brain of the developing infant from that of the adult is the degree to which injury can be sustained in the very young often without the deleterious effects usually associated with such injury. If damage occurs then a large degree of substitution of one area for another is possible in the very young. It is as though the brain has not fully crystallised its pattern of action.

It may happen that one half of the brain is damaged during infancy either through birth injury, something quite common some years back but now relatively rare due to increased standards of obstetrical care, because a young child has had a serious accident, or disease even at that early age has invaded the brain. If the child does have a seriously damaged hemisphere then it is the healthy hemisphere which ultimately learns language, and speech and language are laid down within this hemisphere.

The damage, however, must occur quite early on during the infant's life and certainly during childhood. During the first two years of life it does not matter much which hemisphere has been damaged. Speech can develop in a healthy hemisphere whether it be the left half of the brain or the right.

As the child gets older, however, the situation changes. The opportunity for extensive learning has already occurred and much of the speech has become crystallised and focussed through use and learning in a convenient part of the brain. If the child had matured to the point that the speech process through learning has been laid down and lateralized but the child still has not reached the age of ten, then damage to the left half of the brain usually has a severe effect upon language in most children. This apparently marks the final crystallisation of language at the left hemisphere. At the same time the child under ten years of age who has a severely damaged right hemisphere has a 50 percent chance that he also will show severe speech defects as the result of the damage. Even up to the age of ten, therefore, lateralisation is proceeding slowly and the left hemisphere becomes more and more important for this. The infant brain obviously differs from the adult brain and one important idea which has been put forward as an explanation for the plasticity of the infant brain is that the brain is, so to speak, unconnected.

If the brain can be disconnected by surgery and if the damaged brain can reestablish communication between different parts, then it can be assumed that connecting up of parts is something which comes about as the individual gets older. At first the brain is not strongly connected but over the passage of time and under the influence of learning and overlearning, it gradually becomes more connected. We know from studies of developmental neurology that this idea must to some extent be true because although nerve connections may exist, a true functional connection occurs after myelination when the nerve fibres have fully developed and are coated with their fatty insulating sheath. In all probability in embryonic life the brain may well be largely a functionally disconnected organ. From infancy on, connecting up of the parts will proceed apace but even then it is possible that the very young child has a brain which exists only in the stages of partial connection.

Figure 7. Child's drawing, age four.

The areas which are the oldest in evolutionary terms may function relatively early on in embryonic existence and exert a prior control of behaviour because they function when other parts do not. If the cortex comes into play later as an organ responsible for learning about the world, then it is the cortex which could complete the development. In other words, if different brain areas mature at different times then as the functions of one area are laid down, another part of the brain becomes available. Development is phased in with the periods of learning. The cortex as an organ of learning becomes available at the time when it is most needed, in early infancy when most learning has to be accomplished.

Brain Disorder in Infancy

Some of the most challenging problems are to be encountered in the study of childhood disorder where there is an obvious failure or abnormality of neuropsychological development possibly transitory but often persisting to exert an effect upon the whole range of subsequent behaviour. Many of these childhood disorders are associated with abnormalities of brain function but some occur in the absence of any demonstrable pathology and although often it may be suspected that such pathology exists, the methods capable of revealing it have not yet been developed.

Neuropsychological disorders, wherever they occur and at whatever age they occur, can be extremely serious and place the individual at a great disadvantage. Disorders in children have an extra dimension, however, because they occur early in the life of the individual and can leave that person in a state of disablement for the rest of his life. In addition, neuropsychological disorders frequently interfere with normal development, this may mean that the child is prevented by the disorder from passing through the normal stages such that when he recovers from the disorder he may be at such a disadvantage in the maturation of emotional, intellectual, and mental development that the course of his subsequent development is seriously retarded. The study of childhood disorder is a vast area in which physicians, educators, psychiatrists, psychologists, and therapists of all types are engaged and it is possible here to mention only briefly some of the problems associated with known or suspected damage occurring to the brain.

Something of the problem of what happens when brain abnormality is present in the young child can be seen by analogy with what happens when a child is born deaf. In this disturbance the child does not hear language and consequently learning of patterns of communication through speech is non-existent unless special training is undertaken.

The deaf child, because of a failure to hear the sounds of spoken language, fails to speak and, of course, the one severe defect follows as a consequence of the other. The example of deafness is perhaps one of the most obvious. Yet what happens in the case of deafness can also happen in the case of any of the constructive abilities and faculties that the brain controls, and as with deafness not only may there be a failure of development in the ability affected but there may be failure of development in other areas as well. It is clear also that although abnormalities of gross physical structure as in the case of a tumour or gross disturbance of electrical activity as occurs in epilepsy can be detected, nevertheless disorders of functioning systems in which the brain shows a delicate imbalance but none of these gross symptoms are as yet almost impossible to detect. If we inspect the inside of a radio we may be able to see that a component has been destroyed but usually nothing will be visible to ordinary inspection, yet a fault in the mechanism clearly exists. A similar position pertains to the disorders of the brain. Subtle changes which may lie at the root of severe disorders are at present almost undetectable and yet we have good reason to believe that such disorders do, in fact, exist.

As the child without remedial help who is deaf is severely handicapped from infancy onwards because the hearing system has been damaged, so pathology acting on the nervous system will have similar effects. We may, however, have to await a more sophisticated knowledge of brain engineering before we can specify in any exact detail the nature of the effects.

Behaviour Problems

A number of children present severe behaviour problems. Often it is found that such children show distinct abnormalities in the electrical rhythms of the brain. Children who are restless, who show little in the way of learning ability, and who can attend to any one thing only for a short period of time, may show some abnormality in the electrical rhythms of the brain.

As an illustration of this we can quote the case of a four-year-old child who was the grandson of a doctor. This child was difficult—showed little learning capacity and was highly distractable. This child had one single convulsion. The child was exceptionally restless and never continued with one activity any longer than a few minutes. He was taken for an EEG examination which showed that there were lots of spike and wave changes taking place and that the record persisted as normal only for brief intervals of time.

It was clear that this child had a brain abnormality which was severely affecting his behaviour, making it impossible for him to learn in the ordinary course of events, and significantly and severely delaying his intellectual development. In this case the outcome was a happy one because the child was treated with drugs which had the effect of suppressing the brain abnormality. He then became calm, showed good attention and concentration, and was from then on able to develop in an entirely normal way.

Encephalitis

The way in which children's behaviour can become seriously disturbed by disease processes which affect the brain is also illustrated in cases of encephalitis. This appeared as a new disease in epidemic form as the result of a mysterious infective agent which produced a variety of neurological symptoms and a number of psychiatric ones including tics, mannerisms, compulsions, and obsessions. Although the symptoms are clear the virus was not found and the agent responsible still remains a mystery.

The disease began as an epidemic in the early part of this century. A number of cases were described in Vienna as they occurred between 1916 and 1917. The first cases began to appear in Roumania in the winter of 1915-1916. It then began to spread from one country to another; cases began to be reported mostly in the winter months. The incidence of the disease was greatest in people ages ten to thirty. Between the years 1916 and 1918 there was a progressive spreading of the disease throughout all the major European countries. Cases began to appear in the states and by 1920 the disease was spread worldwide.

A peak was reached in 1920 and a new even higher peak in 1926. The spread of this mysterious epidemic took place over the course of less than ten years. The disease came to worldwide attention in a spectacular manner and then slowly and equally mysteriously the epidemic began to decline. The disease lost its epidemic qualities and although individual cases still occur spasmodically no fresh major outbreaks have been recorded for many years.

The tragic feature of the disease is not so much that it produces an exaggerated representation of the personality, that it induces a true personality change, but that psychiatric disturbance remains in a proportion of the cases after the acute phase has passed.

It was noted that after passing through the acute phase of the infection the child began to behave very badly. In children ages three to ten, there was a great deal of destructiveness and the children acted upon every impulse, however disastrous and ill-conceived. Children who had previously been normal would now lie, steal, destroy property, set fire to things, and commit various sexual offences without thought of punishment. They were markedly unstable and highly aggressive towards others. The patients mutilated themselves on occasion. The children were apparently deeply sorry for what they had done and showed by their feelings that they were by no means deficient in a capacity for remorse at their actions, but they became slaves to what they were doing and were compelled onwards towards destructive acts.

Disorders which infect the brain of children represent a severe condition indeed. The worst feature of the disorder is not necessarily the behavioural complication but the residual effect which may remain as a disturbance of the child's capacity for mental function. In some children the infective agent may act upon the brain in such a severe fashion that much of the intellectual equipment of the child is destroyed placing that child in a state of permanent mental enfeeblement.

Learning Disorder

Children's learning has long been a major concern of the developmental psychologist. It is important to know something of the mechanism and the stages which children pass through in learning in order that it may be possible to teach them effectively. Intensive study of learning, as well as what can go wrong during learning, is also important because the cause of reference to child guidance clinics is the fact that the child is experiencing difficulty at school. Difficulty, it may be said, which is frequently associated with a failure to make progress and a failure to learn through the usual means. The feeling that many children are not achieving their full potential and also that those with learning difficulties need more care and attention is a continuous spur to effort in this area.

By far the most common type of learning difficulty is that experienced in learning to read. Estimates of the incidence of reading difficulty vary quite widely but can often be as high as 10 percent even among children of average intelligence. That inability to read can follow as a consequence of brain damage has been known since 1836 when Lordot described his own inability to read as the result of a brain injury. In many cases inability to read accompanies brain damage and the child may not only be unable to read but speech may also be disturbed. The child may have difficulty in finding the correct words, speech may be inarticulate, and there may be other neurological signs. In such cases it commonly happens that the brain is damaged either at birth because of trauma or because the baby has received insufficient oxygen, or as the result of accident occurring to the brain at a later time but still during early infancy. It also happens frequently that learning disabilities occur in children denied the proper opportunity for learning or because the child has been made so anxious by home or school circumstances. Any severe psychological problem which confronts the child can have an effect on the progress which that child makes with reading. Some authors are inclined to attribute the vast majority of reading difficulties to factors of this sort.

We have to allow, however, that there can be reading disabilities which are associated with pathology of the brain. Even where there are no obvious signs of brain damage, we should point out the fallacy of supposing that brain damage does not exist. Brain damage of restricted extent, not evident to casual inspection, could affect a small part of the total repertoire of behaviour which the individual shows. The fact that other neurological signs are not present does not rule out the possibility of damage to areas vital, for example, to the capacity in learning to read.

In one class of disorders, in which the capacity to learn to read is impaired, there is an inability to deal with letters and words as symbols and this is accompanied by an inability to comprehend the meaningfulness of written material. The problem appears to reflect a basic disturbance of neurological organisation. It is entirely consistent with what we know of the brain that there could be a failure of development or a disturbance of those areas of the brain concerned with integrating visual information with speech and language without other resultant neurological effects. A mysterious defect of this kind exists called specific dyslexia, sometimes described as "word blindness," essentially characterised by an inability to read words.

The first discovery of what was known then as congenital word blindness and now as a specific dyslexia caused considerable interest. Although little is known about the mechanisms involved it seems likely that the disorder results not directly from malfunction of visual perception, although some patients do have disorders in visual perception. Individuals with specific dyslexia for the most part can perceive well. Neither is the disorder centred primarily in the speech systems because individuals can use spoken language without necessary evidence of impairment, although on occasion the speech system can be involved. The most likely system to be implicated is that connecting up the parts of word perception with those of the speech output system. If there is a failure here then what the child perceives cannot be labelled and identified in terms of words although the child can obviously perceive and identify in other ways.

Although there may be an absence of gross abnormalities of a

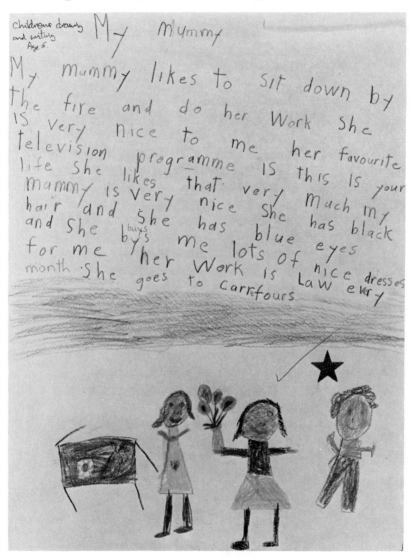

Figure 8. Child's drawing and writing, age 6.

neurological kind associated with the syndrome of specific dyslexia, at the same time there are many signs which indicate a
physical basis for the condition, signs which strongly suggest
that the brain is not working quite as it should. Modern research on this problem shows that in children who have this
condition there is a slowness of ordinary speech development.
The child speaks normally but the onset of speech is delayed. It
is also the case that members of their families are likely to have
reading and spelling difficulties suggesting a constitutional
difficulty persisting from one generation to the next. The
children who have specific dyslexia are more clumsy than
normal children and they confuse directions more easily, for
example, left and right.

All in all, these results support the view that there is a constitutional defect which, although unaccompanied by gross neurological abnormalities, does nevertheless have sufficient
indications of physical disturbance to suggest a developmental anomaly occurring because the brain is constructed as it
is.

Childhood Autism

There are many other disorders which affect children
seriously and delay their intellectual development profoundly
and in all probability are related to abnormalities of function
of the brain, but the relationship, if any, is not as yet clearly
established. Typical of instances of this type are some of the
more severe disorders of childhood which some people regard
as being precipitated by social conditions but could well in
time turn out to be the result of an abnormality of brain
function in the way that physical and psychological symptoms
of encephalitis are clearly dependent upon physical pathology.
The state of childhood autism, for example, is a profoundly
distressing condition in which a variety of severe behaviour
disorders develop.

The condition was originally described as childhood schizophrenia but now a specific variety of this is recognized as
autism. The pattern can be variable but there is a failure to

proceed through the normal stages of childhood development. Some children are withdrawn and passive, whereas others are brilliantly articulate and apparently gifted. We have mentioned the problems which develop out of the fact that a child has been born deaf, the primary problems of deafness and the secondary problems of communication. It follows equally that parts of the brain which deal with communication in failing to function properly can exert an equally profound effect, if not more so, than that of primary deafness. One of the major symptoms of the autistic child is a failure to communicate with others—parents, brothers, sisters, friends.

Parents frequently seek help and guidance in the first instance because the child seems uncomprehending and largely ignores their presence. If, for example, the parent speaks to the child, the child may behave as if he heard nothing. It is almost as though the child is deaf but the child is obviously not deaf, if a familiar tune is played on the record player, although the child is not looking in that direction, he will turn and listen with rapt attention and perhaps move rhythmically or beat time to the record. The inability to communicate with others is a feature which profoundly affects the relationship which the child holds to the mother. Some people single this relationship out as a disturbed one and seek in it the cause of the disorder. It has to be remembered, however, that if the child is disturbed in its capacity to communicate with others and to create a relationship with them, because the mother plays such an important part in the earliest years, she will be the one most likely to notice the disturbance and to be most affected of all the family by it. The child, for example, may show none of the usual anticipations to nursing, e.g. adopting the nursing posture. The child may not reach out to the mother in the usual affectionate relationship. The child may show no sign of the usual smiling response.

Mothers describe the infant's behaviour in the following ways: "I could never reach my baby." "He never smiled at me." "The minute she could walk she ran away from me." "It hurt me so when I saw other babies glad to be in their mothers' arms; my boy always tried to creep away from my lap as soon as he could." "He never greeted me when I entered, he never cried or even noticed when I left the room." "She never was a cuddly baby, she never liked to be caressed, she did not want anybody to embrace or to kiss her. She never made any personal appeal for help at any time."

It is clear from these accounts that the behaviour patterns which usually appear in early infancy—smiling, reaching out to the mother, etc.—may fail to develop in the autistic child. This in itself suggests some fundamental pathology of neuro-psychological organisation because many of these patterns are themselves not learned but follow as a consequence of matura-tion. Even the child born blind smiles at contact with the mother, although, of course, the child is totally unable to see the mother. Children also do not as a rule reject the mother even though she may treat them badly. Something other than simple maternal rejection is at work. Symptoms which are typical of this condition, the classical features as described by Kanner, in addition to the lack of emotional response and the lack of communication are the desire after sameness and the desire for familiar things—a stereotyped preoccupation with a few inanimate objects or actions and an intolerance of change in the surroundings.

Other features are the child's intelligent, even pensive facial expression, in spite of the fact that he does not focus but seems to look through you, and his apparent self-contentedness if left alone. Language suffers very severely, either the children are mute or language is used largely in an inanimate way, for example, as a series of commands to adults, to serve in an executive fashion rather like a switch or the lever of a machine used for the purpose of the child.

The whole complex of the disorder is a mystifying assembly of symptoms, principal of which is this basic disorder of com-munication and affection. In much of the writing on the au-tistic child the impression is given of a sphinxlike infant who struggles against human contact, as though the very contact with parents and other individuals is painful to him. It is said that this is an archaic defence—a negativism and an act of warding off human relationships. It is surely in this that the

Table II

Comparison of Autistic and Psychotic Children on Several Items from Rimland's Diagnostic Checklist*

Item	Autistic, % Speaking n = 65	Autistic, % Mute n = 53	Nonautistic, % n = 230
Did you ever suspect the child was very nearly deaf?			
1 Yes	77	94	54
2 No	23	6	46
	100	100	100
(Age 2-5) Is he cuddly?			
1 Definitely, likes to cling to adults	2	2	20
2 Above average (likes to be held)	8	8	18
3 No, rather stiff and awkward to hold	90	88	56
4 Don't know	0	2	6
	100	100	100
(Age 3-5) How skillful is the child in doing fine work with his fingers or playing with small objects?			
1 Exceptionally skillful	71	75	33
2 Average for age	6	9	23
3 A little awkward, or very awkward	15	8	33
4 Don't know	8	8	11
	100	100	100
(Age 3-5) How interested is the child in mechanical objects such as the stove or vacuum cleaner?			
1 Little or no interest	19	9	23
2 Average interest	4	0	21
3 Fascinated by certain mechanical things	77	91	56
	100	100	100
(Age 3-5) Does child get very upset if certain things he is used to are changed (like furniture or toy arrangement, or certain doors which must be left open or shut)?			
1 No	4	2	29
2 Yes, definitely	87	86	41
3 Slightly true	9	12	30
	100	100	100
(Age 3-5) Does the child typically say "Yes" by repeating the same question he has been asked? (Example: You ask, "Shall we go for a walk, Honey?" and he indicates he does want to by saying, "Shall we go for a walk, Honey?" or "Shall we go for a walk?")			
1 Yes, definitely, does not say "yes" directly	94	12†	22
2 No, would say "Yes" or "OK" or similar answer	0	3	8
3 Not sure	4	6	8
4 Too little speech to say	2	79	62
	100	100	100

* From Gerald C. Davison and John M. Neale, *Abnormal Psychology: An Experimental-Clinical Approach,* 1974. Courtesy of John Wiley & Sons, Inc., New York.

† Speech item not applicable to the mute group.

danger lies. Most of us respond warmly and naturally to the smile of the young baby. At times the baby cries, and the normal infant gets cross and becomes opposed to the mother, and the mother gets cross and resentful against the infant, but all is resolved when the child smiles and responds to an affectionate embrace. If a child lacks these means of expression then an element goes out of the relationship.

Even well-meaning psychiatrists can find themselves at a loss when confronted with children of this kind and this explains something of the rather hostile psychoanalytic interpretation of this condition. If it is possible to treat the symptoms in a more dispassionate way—to employ interpretations more in line with a neuropsychological emphasis—it may be beneficial. For example, is the child showing negativism or hostility towards the mother in failing to smile at her or is it simply that these behaviour patterns have failed to develop? If the child ignores the parent as a source of stimulation and yet attends to an old familiar record played on the record player, then this is certainly abnormal, but is it an acquired psychic defence or an attempt to shut down the more varying stimulation of the world and to respond only to those aspects which are well-learned and familiar? The need to cling to stability and to preserve things as the same would suggest that it may be the latter.

Certainly, if it is possible to interpret the disorder in terms of underlying failure of brain mechanisms then this will be an important step in the understanding of the nature of childhood disorders of this type. The abnormalities are such as to make it extremely probable that there is some physical basis to them and an important research effort must be directed towards discovering what this physical basis is.

Chapter VII

THE NORMAL BRAIN

Views of the Brain

THROUGHOUT the history of the study of the human brain, we have witnessed a variety of interpretations as to the nature and the mode of its functions. To the ancients the connection between brain and behaviour was often not appreciated or appreciated only dimly. Even in the times of Aristotle, the view was expressed that the brain was little more than a cooling system and the presence of mucous descending to the nose was taken to indicate the fact that the brain was at work. Other views were that there were temperaments controlled by four humers or fluids which circulated around the brain and other organs. Another view was that there was a worm or "vermis" in the brain which had the important function of regulating the passage of fluid across the brain.

It is to Gall and Spurzheim we have to turn, however, for ideas of cerebral localisation and the origin of the school of phrenology which supposed that the attributes of the personality could be related to the various parts of the brain and that if the brain should develop a particular facility then this would result in an expansion of the brain beneath and a development of an observable protrusion of the skull above. We now know that phrenology is not an acceptable theory of how the brain functions. Not only is it inaccurate to divide up the attributes of the person into the categories which Gall and Spurzheim used—in other words the classification of abilities was spurious—but also there is no reason to suppose that the development of a particular ability necessarily leads to or accompanies an actual increase in the physical size of that region of the brain or for that matter that there is a physical correspondence between the contour features of the brain beneath and those of the skull above. The skull may not in fact reflect the shapings of the brain even in that area directly below it. Phrenology is important, however, in that it suggested the idea of the localisation of abilities in the human brain and it is this to which we owe a considerable debt. Those early views of the functioning of the brain are of little contemporary practical significance but to study them is salutary in that they indicate to us that what we may believe today can in the fullness of time come to be replaced by a more full and detailed knowledge of a more accurate kind which may be something completely different from what we now believe. The picture clearly changes as more and more evidence becomes available, enabling us to reject some notions and at the same time to cling to others.

One more modern view of the brain is that it is in essence a special kind of telephone exchange in which connections and disconnections are established between adjacent or remote portions. This view was proposed as the result of some of the original investigations on the nature of connecting fibres between one part of the brain and another. It became known that the brain does in fact transmit information around its interior and that the brain is not, therefore, a passive assembly of different regions each speaking with its own voice but a network or unified system brought into a harmonious relationship by the communications which exist within it.

Arising out of this view of the brain as an interconnected network, perhaps in some respects resembling that of a sophisticated telephone exchange, has grown the important study which investigates the brain of man as though he were a communications channel—which in many respects he obviously is.

As an example of this let us take the typist described earlier who working in her office looks at the written page, takes the information she sees there into her brain, and then with a facility which can only be described as remarkable, translates what she sees as shorthand or written script through the medium of the typewriter into immaculately typed scripts. The important question is how is it possible for her to do this at all. In one sense she is acting as a channel for the transmission of information. We can check on the efficiency of the typist in dealing with the information which passes through her brain by looking at what she has to type and by seeing what she actually has typed, to find errors and also to see how quickly her brain can accomplish the amount of work which she has been given to do.

Therefore, an important way of studying the functions of the brain, both in health and in disease, is to study the capacity of that brain for communication. When damage is inflicted upon the brain it is clear that this capacity to transmit information from one source to another is severely impaired because the equipment of the brain necessary for this and the channels by which information is passed around the brain may have been destroyed.

Important theories exist of the brain as an information channel. There are limits, however, to the speed at which the brain can work in this way. This is clear from our example of the work which the typist is called on to perform. The busy typist who is called on to do a lot more additional work is liable to fail or burst into tears with a resulting disruption of the work which is already in progress. In experimental studies of the brain it is found that a person has great difficulty in doing two tasks at the same time, particularly where both require a great deal of participation. What usually happens is that part of one task is held in the memory store whilst part of the other task is completed and so the brain proceeds piecemeal. If, for example, a person is given a signal for a response, a light flashes and he is to respond as quickly as possible to this, then if he is given very very quickly afterwards another signal to respond, his response to the second signal will be very protracted and delayed. It is argued that the brain whilst analysing one signal cannot simultaneously be employed in the analysis of another signal. In the well-known experiments in which two messages are played at the same time one to one ear and the other to the other, the person responds to one message of the two and holds the other message in memory for subsequent response.

All this suggests that the brain acts as a communication channel, but like a communication channel it has only a limited capacity and not all the information can pass through at once. It has been suggested that the brain consists of only one channel and that this is the reason for the delay and hold-up in the processing of multiple pieces of information. Not all the evidence has supported such a view, however, and particularly where information is channelled in separate streams into the cerebral hemispheres there is evidence that the brain can deal with multiple strands of information in parallel, or as two computers lying side by side in the brain.

It is clear, however, that the view of the brain as a communication channel has been and still is a powerful theory generating much research. At the same time the brain is far more than a passive receiver and transmitter of information. The fact that it is a communication channel is beyond dispute—but this is one facet of the work of the brain and only one facet of the total of functions which it performs. Emphasis indeed has moved from the consideration of the brain as just a channel of communication to the brain as a decision mechanism. One theory is that it acts as something of a statistical machine dealing with a world in which events are not always certain and in which in order to plan for the future it is necessary to some extent to guess what is likely to happen on the basis of information which is itself not certain and in some measure unpredictable. Such a theory of the working of the brain is known as the statistical decision theory. The situation could be said to resemble that of the investor on the stock market—an individual who is attempting to do his best to increase the value of what money he has in a risky and uncertain world. He can only guess on the basis of what information he can gather as to the course of future events. The brain it is said, faced with considerable uncertainty, is likewise a device which acts to guess about the outcome of events and the part the individual should play in those events. Once again, theories of this kind which are important in their own right can be said to represent only some facets of what the brain does. The problem of identifying the overall functions and gaining a vision of the workings of the brain in any more than a piecemeal fashion represents a daunting task which psychology no doubt will aspire to solve over the years but it is at the same time something which at present is not totally within our grasp.

The emphasis upon the decision processes of the brain has suggested to many that the brain might work in some respects like a modern computer, and of course in some ways the analogy is particularly apt. The brain has a highly complex intake and output. We can only suppose that the method of its function is based upon logical principles, possibly similar to those employed in computing. Some of the actions of the brain can be modelled upon a computer. It is also possible to construct artificial intelligence systems capable, for example, of playing chess, thus suggesting analogies with the working of the brain. The disciplines of cybernetics, which ostensibly means the study of control and feedback mechanisms and the study of artificial intelligence, if they tell us nothing at all directly about the human brain, do tell us about artificial brains and those features by which, given the particular circumstances and the technology, it is possible to design a brain.

The tracing of the way in which concepts of the brain have been influenced by contemporary technology as it exists at any one historical period represents a fascinating study in itself. However, caution should be exercised in taking the fruits of contemporary technology and translating these directly as a model for the workings of the brain. Once again the lesson of history is a salutary one for as each new technology replaces the old, insights which may have been gained have to be set against the inaccuracies which premature overembracing may involve. We may need to restrict our sights and concentrate on gaining accurate and detailed knowledge of a direct kind rather than prematurely adopt synthetic systems as indubitably representing the action of the brain when this may not be the case.

History shows that previous technologies have not provided as accurate a model as people supposed. We may be in great danger of regarding the brain as a cooling system in our own terms. In order to know if a given model represents the working of the brain, we need fundamental and accurate knowledge which can only be gained by detailed and painstaking research. Neuropsychology has one fundamental aim from which it should not be deflected into the byways of interpretative technology, and that is to understand and promote the workings of the human brain. It is arguable that this aim is fulfilled by the study of cooling systems, telephone exchanges, and information systems, or even modern computers, yet at the same time it would be foolish to deny the impact of technologies of this kind if even to provide a framework for thought.

In a book which deals with the subject matter of neuropsychology it is our opinion that studies of the action of the normal brain should find a prominent place. There is much research in progress to be brought to the attention of the discerning reader. The study of psychology has as its specific aim the understanding of psychological processes as they occur in the normal individual. Psychology is widely regarded as the basic science of the study of behaviour and experience whereas psychiatry has an implicit concern with the abnormalities of behaviour, experience, or mind. Although basic neurology is concerned with the fundamental science of workings of the brain, many neurologists confine themselves to clinical practice and their interest lies in obtaining information with the cure of a disability as its aim. It is entirely appropriate therefore, that the subject of psychology should deal with those abilities, however expressed, which characterise the normal individual without any surreptitious looking over the shoulder at clinical material, and without exclusive reliance upon cases involving a damaged or disordered brain or those where some intellectual processes are disturbed by disease or mental illness however caused. The study of the capacities of the normal brain must therefore occupy a place in the study of neuropsychology and attention must devolve on the crucial problem of the part played by the brain in the origin, control, and genesis of psychological functions as they occur in normal man.

The traditional study of the psychological processes of the brain-damaged individual has as one of its direct aims, and some would argue its most important aim, the understanding of the workings of the brain in health and in disease. The effects of damage to the brain are regarded in this sense as enlightening facets of everyday performance which cannot be so illuminated by studies of normal individuals. If we argue that some large part of neuropsychology must by its very nature be devoted to a study of those psychological processes of the abnormal brain, then it is possible to establish the effects of that abnormality only by comparison with what happens in the "normal" case. The study of the effects of brain damage and abnormality proceeds hand in hand with the study of the normal brain and presupposes such an investigation. Normality and abnormality are locked together like Siamese twins. The fact is that the study of normality and abnormality are caught together in the meshes of the scientific net. The abnormal is by definition that which is not normal, something which can only be studied by reference to the normal. The study of the abnormal is capable of illuminating the working of the brain often in a surprising and dramatic way, hence it must be regarded as indispensible to the basic science of the study of the brain. However, it must still be emphasized that the drama of this is revealed only by virtue of the fact that explicit and implicit standards are available by which behaviour itself can be judged, and these standards are those of the "normal" individual.

Internal Working

We can make an analogy to a watch which works by a simple mechanism which is well understood. The watch can be seen to display its functions and we know that it is working if we hear it tick or if we see the hands move around the face. That there is a internal mechanism responsible for this is clear. That the mechanism is not just a collection of cogs pushed haphazardly into the casing of the watch is equally clear. What happens for the timepiece is something which also happens in the brain. The brain is an intricate mechanism in which the parts are brought together in a finely balanced working relationship. It is the character of this working relationship which is our explicit concern. The brain embraces and encapsulates these various functions and within the brain there is a complete world of enmeshing relationships which is difficult to spell out because we are lacking in information. The realm of function is something more than the physical parts or the anatomical regions of the brain. There is a plan of action whereby human function is governed by the intricate interrelationship of the parts of the brain—as the hands of the watch pursue their course under the governance of the relationship between the parts of the mechanism inside.

Frequently this area of function is described as pertaining to the mind, i.e. the mind is used as the term to embrace such functional relationships. The term "mind" can, of course, be used in a nonphysical sense to refer not to this realm of function at all but to the mental world, the workings of experience and consciousness, an unrelated realm and something not referrent to the physical action of the brain. It can also be used to refer to the functional relationships of the brain but the investigator through the use of this confusing terminology is often led to talk about different things as though they were the same.

Perhaps we should seek a different approach, possibly one in analogy with the great Eastern desert houses, the "caravanserai," where there exists within the natural world a tiny miniature physical world having a correspondence to the world outside and yet essentially regulated by the principles operating from the elements within. Commerce with the outside is possible but this is arranged through the working of the intrinsic internal order. There is a physical relationship between brain, behaviour, and psychological processes. The mechanism has to exist in a subtle working relationship before it can function. A kind of intrinsic perfection is essential, there must be a subtle interplay of forces.

The brain has its own physical world and there are conditions to be fulfilled in order that the functions can appear in a smooth regular fashion. None of these processes are necessarily mental and yet it is clear that the mere description alone of the pieces which go to make up the machinery is inadequate to allow us to understand the nature of the function. There is a world of description, a realm of intricate skill through which the parts are brought to life. That this is essentially a physical process demanding no laying on of hands or invoking of spirits is illustrated by the fact that similar problems are encountered in the mechanical world, for example, in the construction of a watch or electronic instrument where all the processes can be described and the technology transmitted from one craftsman to another. There is domain in which the functioning machinery resides where the accurate functioning of the individual as we know him exists and is laid down. Here we enter a special province, a unique world of complexity, not a haphazard assembly of physical parts but a realm of complex interrelationships, a new territory or content encapsulated from the world but in contact with the world—the caravanserai of the brain. The caravanserai has its own internal organisation and it is only through this that it maintains an active transport with the world around it. The caravanserai also is an enclosure or envelope which has the important quality of being to some degree separate from the rest of the world. It is more than a physical structure existing in isolation in a desert, it is an active working community and as such it bears analogy to the brain.

It seems strange to us now that at one time it was not known that the brain is composed of small functional units or cells. We have become so used to thinking of the brain in this way. If we remember that beneath each square centimetre of cortex there are at least five million cells and probably more, then it can be seen that the job of tracing through the exact number of connections is a very complicated one indeed and a venture with which the neuropsychologist cannot as yet contend. However, already we know much about the functioning of individual cells, at least as they play their part within the network of the brain, and in the fullness of time it may well be that the brain-behaviour relationship with which the neuropsychologist is so concerned will be studied more and more with the functioning of individual cells, or at least very small groups of cells, in mind and will have as its explicit purpose the study of the relationship which they hold to behaviour. For the present, however, although important work is in progress on the functioning of single cells, our effort is concentrated on the action of the brain as concerns the larger mass of its tissue.

Brain Size

One remarkable feature of the normal human brain is the size which ultimately it attains. In many respects the brain is a big organ. This may not be all that surprising when we consider the complexity and multitudinous nature of the functions which it has to perform. Certainly it is a compact unit for what it does. The elements which make its function possible are closely packed to form a fine network of interlocking cells. It is indeed remarkable that so much can be achieved by a mass of grey tissue weighing a couple of pounds. The microminiaturisation of the brain is something quite unparalleled. It is estimated that there may be more cells in the human brain than grains of sand on the beach or even stars in the galaxy. Thus in the normal human brain the functioning elements are connected and interconnected into dense networks. It is this fabric, the enchanted loom as Sherrington called it, which gives the brain its unique quality.

One unique feature is the total size which the brain ultimately attains. If, it is argued, the productive machinery resides in the cells, the working elements of the brain, then the argument would follow that the larger the number of cells or the bigger the brain, the greater creative capacity that brain will have. If we study the evolution of the brain in its development from a primitive form to the brain of man then it is clear that there has been a progressive increase in size and that the brain of man is composed of a very large agglomeration of cells indeed.

However, the actual size is not the only feature which distinguishes the human brain; the brain of man in fact is not the largest known organ. The brain of the elephant is somewhat larger than the human brain. Animals with a very heavy brain usually have large bodies and the development of the size of the brain is to some degree related to the bulk of body which has to be controlled by that brain. Although the brain of man is large, it is also the case that the ratio of the brain to the size of the body in man is very large, i.e. there is a lot of brain in comparison to the total amount of body. Nonetheless, this factor is not a unique one. The brain-body ratio of some monkeys is higher than that for man and so clearly this is not a feature which uniquely distinguishes him from representative members of the animal kingdom, although it is an important feature nonetheless. The weight of the brain of the woman is somewhat less than that of the brain of the man. Antifeminists have made much of this but it appears that this difference can be explained almost entirely on the grounds that women have a smaller body and their brain is proportionately less in size to conform with this diminished size.

Although we have argued that large brains make for elevated behaviour, in man the situation is rather paradoxical because when the brain of a genius has been studied at postmortem, it has seldom been found that men of genius have a brain size which is increased greatly over that of the members of the general public. Another fact is that on occasion individuals are born who are in possession not only of a very small head but also an exceptionally small brain inside it; other aspects, for example their physical stature, may be normal. This is a clinical condition know as microcephaly; such people although categorised as mentally subnormal are not usually the most severely subnormal in spite of the smallness of the brain. They may well have capacities for work and for talk and often considerable conversational powers. Individuals do, therefore, exist who have brains remarkably scaled down in size and although there is obvious deficit, the disadvantage to these individuals is not as severe as may have been judged from a knowledge of their brain size alone.

At the other pole, there are those individuals with exceptionally large brains. There have been cases, for example, of individuals in whom two brains have developed, one on top of the other, and the two have fused in an intricate relationship. Such people are freaks and usually such abnormality of brain is accompanied not by double brain power but by gross mental subnormality because the necessary arrangements of the brain are disrupted and the brain fails to work as an effective organ. It is clear that in considering the physical organisation of the brain there is more to the production of intelligent behaviour than just the size which the brain attains. Yet this must at the same time be viewed against the evolutionary background of the brain which demonstrates that an organ increases progressively in size as new realms of complex and intelligent behaviour become available to the species as it ascends the evolutionary scale. The same holds true for the evolutionary history of man and we can only assume that the development of man's civilisation indicates that the complexity and level of his intelligent behaviour has increased.

Whether the brain as an organ in man's intelligent conduct continues on a course of evolution is hard to say. It has been argued that the forces which once operated to ensure the propagation of brain power because it was useful in promoting the survival of the fittest no longer pertain. If this is true, it may mean that man has residing in his brain codes for behaviour which are at best neutral to the question of survival or at worst contain the seeds of his own destruction. If this is not true then the brain still may well be set on a course of evolution and change and who can predict what the ultimate shape of the human abilities and conduct may become.

One thing is certain, however, that the aggregation of more and more cells to increase the mere size of the brain may not prove to be the answer if by aggregation there is a destruction of the already existing functional organisation of the brain. A brain continuing to evolve must do so through the change of functional units—progressively substituting one for the other without at the same time rendering the individual hopelessly disabled and incapable of rational thought or more importantly destroying the basic patterns of reproduction and survival in the process. It is probable that there are organisational differences even in the lower structures which distinguish the brain of man from that of the animals. Certainly it is the case, as we have seen, that the brain of man is distinguished by the development of his cerebral cortex which is massive and composed of relatively new tissue which covers the topmost areas of the brain. It is this area which is responsible for the highest processes and this area which maintains for man the fabric of intellect, reason, volition, and will.

Dominance and Control

There is one feature upon which we must comment at this stage and this is expressed as the idea of cerebral dominance in function. One hemisphere of the brain according to this concept prevails in specific function over the other and is thus said to be predominant. It is a question of much interest as to whether the brain reveals anatomical differences between one side and the other which could be said to correlate with this version of cerebral dominance and could form an anatomical basis for what is to be observed in function. For the most part, it is the symmetry and not the asymmetry of the brain which is remarkable. However, in recent years some observations have emerged to suggest that the human brain, in terms of pure anatomy alone, may not on one side be the exact counterpart of the other, although at the same time for the vast extent of its structures, as far as we know, this is so.

The information about hemisphere differences is at present rather sparse. It has been reported that there is a difference in the speed at which the projections cross from the hemisphere to the pyramidal tract. Studies on the developing pyramidal tract show that the projections from the left hemisphere begin to cross before those on the right. Blood supplies upwards to the brain are also reported to be different in right-handed and left-handed people. In addition, it has been reported that in the normal right-handed person an area of the brain concerned with speech occupies a larger volume than at the opposite hemisphere and that this difference is to be observed in the young human infant a long time before speech is possible.

There are, therefore, anatomical differences between one side of the brain and the other as the results of recent research shows. The problem remains as to the exact significance which attaches to these differences. On the whole we tend to emphasise the physical similarity between the two sides of the brain, although at the same time the significance of the differences which do exist must be acknowledged.

That there are some anatomical differences between the cerebral hemispheres is now clear. It is also clear that there are functional differences reflected in performance. Some of these differences can be related to the anatomical differences already described, for example, the differences in speech lateralisation between one hemisphere and another, some other of the differences however cannot and as yet these differences in function between one half of the brain and the other are poorly understood. It is commonly supposed that they arise through a need for the brain to specialise and to divide up its labour between the two halves. There are differences in the performance of the normal brain between one hemisphere and the other and our task is to discuss something of these differences and to describe their meaning.

Some of the asymmetries of the normal brain are revealed first of all in the patterns of handedness which the individual shows. These patterns of body asymmetries are important because they show something about the way in which the brain acts through the body in the production of behaviour. It is commonly thought that the individual is right-handed or left-handed only, but in fact laterality can apply to many regions of the body. The person may be left-footed or right-footed, he may be right-eyed or left-eyed, even the position which his nose occupies upon his face can be turned to the right or to the left.

That the vast majority of the population is right-handed is a fact which almost goes without saying, estimates vary from between 86 percent to 95 percent depending upon the particular tests used. Certainly, most of the population is right-handed and most of the population also is right-eyed. What is the significance of this fact? There is a link between handedness and functions of the individual's brain because the activities of the hand at each side are largely in control of the hemisphere of the brain at the opposite side. A correlation has frequently been made between the functions of the hand, or what the hand can accomplish, and the proficiency of the brain as it operates and the way in which it functions. What the hand can do is regarded as a reflection of the functioning of the brain. Because the vast majority of the population is right-handed and there is no doubt that the right-hand exerts a superiority certainly in penmanship and in other ways, it has been taken that the part of the brain controlling that hand also has a superiority or a functional preeminence and thus this factor became one of significance in the development of ideas about cerebral dominance.

It has been known since the earliest days of neuropsychology that damage to the left hemisphere of the brain impairs the capacity for speech and language. This impairment is no simple thing and can arise from a variety of causes. In the normal brain, however, speech pursues its fluent course, but even here something of the lateralisation of the speech system, even if only for output, makes itself apparent. In generalising from the results of a vast number of experiments which study the capacity of the individual to read or report material flashed to the right or to the left half of the visual field in normal man, and hence to the left or to the right hemisphere, it has been found that response to verbal material on the left hemisphere has been superior to that on the right. Hence normal brain results parallel quite closely those for the brain-damaged individual. In addition, using contact lenses to restrict visual input to the left or right visual field, and hence to the right or left hemisphere, we have recently found that words presented to the left hemisphere are readily understood, typed, and written whereas the right hemisphere takes a long time and experiences great difficulty in reading the words it receives. It is commonly argued that such differences as exist illustrate that in functional terms the brain is left-centered (in the right-handed person) or that it is a "lopsided organ." Speech, for example, is supposed to be the principle master control of the intellectual process, according to this view, and because speech disorders result from damage occurring to the left side of the brain it is supposed that the left hemisphere dominates the rest of the brain through its control over the speech process. Because the vast majority of the population is right-handed this also is taken as an indication of the superiority of the hemisphere which exerts control over the hand and leads towards the view of the left hemisphere being dominant over that of the right.

When only the facts of handedness and speech were known there was little evidence to run counter to the view that in the large majority of the population the left hemisphere was the one which dominated in its control over the right. However, with increasing knowledge of the functions of both sides of the brain and the part played by each, particularly in the normal brain, a picture has emerged by no means as simple as perhaps it was first supposed. It is clear that in the normal brain the specialisms at one side of the brain are matched by other specialisms of the opposite hemisphere.

The modern picture which has emerged is of the brain with different specialisms at each side and this fact, if no other, has resulted in a reduction of the degree to which one is inclined to credit the one hemisphere with unchanging unilateral control over the other. Ideas of cerebral dominance are still important but not as important as they once were and the concept of hierarchic control is often seen as something which can pertain to either hemisphere depending on what abilities the brain is called on to perform at any one time.

Progress in the study of the normal brain has gone along in parallel with that of the study of the behaviour and performance of brain-damaged individuals. We now know far more about the functions of the right hemisphere than we used to. The right hemisphere shows its special realm of function also, for example, it emerges superior in the recognition of the spatial material presented to it. Pictures of faces are recognised better when flashed to the right hemisphere both in the split-brain and in the normal individual. The right hemisphere also appears superior on other tasks concerned with spatial recognition—for example, in the recognition of spatial designs, enumeration of dots, judgement of slant, and distance performance. This work on the normal brain suggests not only that the right hemisphere is of primary importance for complex visuospatial functions but also for more fundamental perceptual processes as well.

Relationship Between Normal and Abnormal Brains

We now have to discuss what the exact relationship is between the functions of the normal brain and what happens in the case of the brain-damaged individual. Evidence from brain-damaged individuals is often taken as an indication of how the normal brain must function. If a given ability is found to be in a severe state of decline following damage to a particular region, it is generally assumed that that part of the brain plays some crucial role in the genesis and control of that ability. This is probably the best working hypothesis but it has to be remembered that what the person can do after surgery or after damage is accomplished by what remains of the rest of his brain and indicates the capacity of the brain to compensate in the face of considerable difficulties.

The comparisons commonly made between the results from brain-damaged individuals and those of normals also may not be deemed to hold universally true, particularly where parts of the brain concerned with èxternal communication to the outside world are concerned. As with the severe spastic quadraplegic patient who, although possessed of a fine intellect, finds it well nigh impossible to communicate with the external world, brain damage as it affects the capacity of the individual to communicate may produce an impression of disability real and genuine enough but which at the same time represents interference with the capacity to communicate and not interference necessarily with the source of mental functioning. It follows from this that studies of the brain-damaged individual may not always be parallel and run hand in hand with those studies of the normal brain. Indeed, in theoretical terms, instances where a lack of correspondence is evident are as important as those where there are close parallels.

It is at those points where the normal brain works according to a different principle than that of the brain-damaged individual that we should look to enquire why the normal brain does not mirror the pattern observed in the case of damage and this can give us insight into what is so special about having a brain intact in which the integrity is preserved. It is here that we can analyse the remarkable facility of the brain to compensate for the damage inflicted upon it. It is this which will give insight into the fluent workings of this incredible organ.

The situation closely resembles that where the electronic engineer finds that a fault has developed in a particular piece of equipment. He is faced with the problem of tracing where the fault may lie. If he is familiar with the pathways which the electrical activity takes through the equipment then his task becomes an easier one because he is able to test different pathways and parts of pathways in turn until he comes to the part of the equipment which shows the fault. He could equally well, if he wished, learn how a piece of equipment acted which was functioning perfectly well and trace through the various channels of the equipment in exactly the same way. He would thus gain considerable insight into the equipment in question. A similar situation pertains in the case of the human brain. If, for example, there is an accurate knowledge of the anatomical pathways which a signal pursues in its passage through the brain it becomes possible by the use of special tests to do something similar to what the electronics engineer does and select which channels or parts of channels are going to be regarded as appropriate for special study. At the moment, for example, the functioning of the cerebral hemispheres can be compared by passing information through the left or right cerebral hemisphere into the rest of the brain through the right or left visual fields. Already it is possible to compare the entry channels into the brain, but it is possible to study the functional significance of these respective entry channels only by virtue of the fact that we have anatomical knowledge of the brain pathways. It is this fusion of knowledge from the fields of anatomy, neuropsychology, and physiology which ultimately will prove to be of widest significance in understanding the mechanisms of the normal brain and the part that these play in the genesis and control of behaviour.

Chapter VIII

PSYCHIATRY

Neuropsychological Approach

ONE of the significant features of neuropsychology is that there is a trend towards the study of mental function as it relates to disorders of the brain rather than through the examination of the mental world unrelated to structure or through psychoanalysis. A neuropsychological programme for the study of psychiatric illness would be one in which psychiatric illness would be investigated to discover abnormalities of the brain which could wholly or in part account for the symptoms and nature of the disturbances typical of the condition. Neuropsychology is allied to those important branches of psychiatry which are concerned with the behavioural effects of disease states of the brain—brain damage, tumour, organic states, senile dementia, etc. Neuropsychology has as one of its aims the discovery of the relationship physical pathology affecting the brain has to behaviour and the structure of mental abilities, not only to assist in the provision of rational forms of therapy based upon knowledge of what the brain can accomplish, although damaged, but also to shed light on the fundamental workings of the human brain both when in health and when afflicted by disease.

There is another important extension of the activities of the subject with which neuropsychology can concern itself, and is now in fact beginning to do so, and that is pioneer investigations into the territory of psychiatry where explanations that the patient's symptoms are due to some physical pathology of the brain are by no means obvious. Neuropsychological techniques, in other words, provide new methods for looking at the functions of the brain, in particular the disruption of function which can exist in psychiatric conditions when this is viewed against the context of the activities of the working brain, des-

149

pite the fact that in many cases direct physiopathological evidence may be absent or only minimally indicative.

Neuropsychology has extended the frontiers of its enquiry, by the application of its own special techniques to psychiatric illnesses not heretofore investigated by these means, to reveal evidence or new symptoms which are relevant to the interpretation of the nature of a disorder in the light of the physical processes of the brain. Neuropsychology is just at the beginning of this venture and it is too early at this stage to comment on the total success of an enquiry of this kind. However, it should be said that neuropsychology represents a new kind of instrument to bring to bear upon the psychiatric disturbances. There would be no point in conducting enquiries as research if at the same time we knew the outcome of this research. Similarly, the search for a physical basis of psychiatric conditions through the use of neuropsychological tools may not always succeed. The important thing is that such a search should prove to be successful in some important respects. It is probably true to say that such a claim can already be made for the use of some of the methods already outlined.

The fact that investigations are made with an aim of discovering whether or not a physical basis can be suggested for certain psychiatric conditions by no means leads to the presupposition that all psychiatric disturbances are to be regarded as due to anomalies of brain function. There are those who may suggest this but the fact that neuropsychology sets itself a programme of research investigating psychiatric states does not imply this nor does the neuropsychological interpretation preclude other types of interpretation which may be placed upon the nature of psychiatric illness.

Neuropsychology now has a very special role to play in psychiatry, a role which is perhaps not as widely recognised within psychiatry itself as it should be but an important one nonetheless. This role is essentially to combat what might be called the physical fallacy based upon the view that a pathologist's report will provide totally comprehensive physical evidence about those processes which operate within the brain to disturb man's psychological functions. The fallacy lies not in this but in the conclusion frequently reached that if the pathologist's report produces no evidence of pathological processes of the brain then that brain is normal in all respects and that the peculiarities, idiosyncracies, and disturbances which the individual shows are not organic, but somehow a functional disorder thrown up by the individual's life experience or through some intrinsic weakness of his psychological organisation. It is not the intention here to imply that there is no such thing as a functional disorder but to question that the absence of known pathology, as indicated by the pathologist's report, necessarily indicates this and also necessarily excludes an organic interpretation. In other words, we question here the meaningful nature of the distinction made so frequently in psychiatric diagnosis between organic and functional states, on the grounds that the pathologist's report indicates gross pathology of the brain when present and thus delineates the organic disorder, and whilst it obviously can do this what it does not do is to exclude anomalies of brain function in those instances where no gross detectable pathology can be found.

The situation in some respects may be regarded as the equivalent of seeking the fault which has developed in a radio and opening up the back and looking inside. If something blows up or wires become loose, then it will be possible to indicate the nature of the damage and to effect some kind of repair. If, however, faults have developed in the units of the set, visual inspection may reveal nothing. It is only by the painstaking testing of each channel of the receiver in turn, the functional approach, that the nature of the.damage will be revealed. Similarly with the brain, it is a mistake to think that all pathology is revealed by inspection even under the microscope. Clearly disturbances of the units of the brain can exist, not revealed to inspection but having an effect upon functioning and working their way through in the expression of the patient's psychological abilities.

Absence of gross pathology should not, therefore, be taken as an absence of organic involvement. This is where neuropsychology comes into its own and this is where neuropsychology has such a special role to play. Neuropsychology is concerned with function, by function we mean the actions, doings, and workings of the brain. We are getting into a tangle here with the terminology and it should be noted that by the use of the term function in this present context we do not mean nonorganic. The neuropsychologist is concerned with testing function and in relating this back to the workings of the brain. The neuropsychologist may well reveal a great deal about the nature of psychiatric disorder as it relates to the gross pathology of the brain, but increasingly in the armament of his skills he is refining techniques to test disorders of function which by the pattern of their existence show the workings of the brain to be disordered according to some pattern which must lie within the fabric of the brain and yet in some instances lies outside of the organic syndromes as determined by known pathology of structure.

Neuropsychology is then spearheading an advance in understanding the workings of the brain in psychiatric disorder which concerns itself with the disorders of function and at the same time suggests that these disorders are not themselves detached from the disturbed workings of the brain but are an expression of it. The analogy again is to complex electronic equipment. Our concern is both with the effect of the loose wire and with the fundamental failure of the intrinsic components of the machine and it is in the investigation of this latter condition that the neuropsychologist has an especially important part to play. No doubt the neuropsychologist in entering upon this area will be accused of "pseudoneurologizing"—that in itself may be not such a bad thing if it allows some new fundamental insight into the brain—but the neuropsychologist is not "pseudoneurologizing," he is bringing a new set of techniques to bear on age-old problems, techniques individual and particular to himself, based upon neurological knowledge and valuable to neurologists but essentially derived from psychological conceptions arising out of the discipline of psychology itself.

There are many approaches to the problems of psychiatric disturbance. A variety of therapies are employed, psychoanalytic, social and behaviourist, drug therapies, and physical therapies. The neuropsychological approach to psychiatric disorders pursues investigations which are at present largely research oriented and aimed at getting initial insights. Although the programme which neuropsychology sets itself to investigate fundamental mechanisms of the brain as they relate to behaviour, is still only in its infancy, and although such a programme does not preclude other interpretations of psychiatric disorder, nonetheless an approach to therapy through neuropsychology is preeminently possible and we are already witness to some developments of this kind taking place.

Depression

Depression is an illness formerly known as melancholia, the chief feature of which is the change of mood which gives the feeling of despair and hopelessness. Undoubtedly some depression occurs as part of everyday life but sometimes the depression becomes so deep that the person suffers a great deal and becomes incapacitated by it. The explanations generally put forward to account for depression are that there is a basic vulnerability and predisposition towards it on the part of the person who suffers from it, that there is a genetic process at work determined by heredity, that early life experiences are important, and, a more recent view, that it results from a failure to cope, a decrease in self-esteem, together with feelings of helplessness to do anything about the life situation.

One of the interesting developments of recent years concerns a remarkable interpretation in terms of the hemisphere functions of the brain. Flor-Henry was responsible for the view that the right hemisphere plays some special role. He studied the emotional behaviour and experiences of patients with damage to the temproral lobe causing them to suffer from epilepsy. His interpretation was that damage to the right hemisphere had different effects from damage to the left hemisphere and that the depressive response was something essentially emerging from the right hemisphere.

Something of the same thing has been reported in studies where sodium amytal is used to inactivate each side of the brain in patients about to have neurosurgery when it is necessary to search for the speech area to make sure that it is preserved and not touched in any way during the surgery. When the left side of the brain is treated in this way, the right hemisphere shows a depressive catastrophic reaction. This finding has been confirmed by several investigators and suggests that depression is something essentially emerging from the right hemisphere of the brain.

Where parts of the brain at each side have been removed or destroyed, then once again we see the right hemisphere playing a major role. Evidence coming from modern psychosurgery suggests that severe depression can be treated by lesioning a large area of the "cingulum" of the right hemisphere. Other studies involving damage to the brain also suggest that the right hemisphere plays some special part in generating the depressive vision of the world and the depressive response to events.

When people are asked questions of an emotional nature which involves them, they consistently look to the left, this is taken as suggesting that the right hemisphere has a special role in emotion in the intact brain. This suggests not only a particular participation of a part of the brain but also the right hemisphere of the brain signalling the state of its emotion by which another person, or the right hemisphere of that person, can be informed about the state of the other. Needless to say, the possibility of the right hemispheres of two people signalling emotion to each other is something which needs extensive investigation.

In the present author's own work a technique has been developed to enable people to see the world through one hemisphere of the brain at a time. This is a contact lens optic system which directs vision either to the right or the left hemisphere. One advantage of this system is that people can walk around the world carrying out everyday tasks, being tested for their psychological functions when all that they see is exclusively channeled to one hemisphere. This is important, of course, because we can compare one hemisphere with the other. There exists, we have discovered, a difference in emotional vision between the two hemispheres.

When films are shown, the right hemisphere sees things as more unpleasant and horrific than the left and its vision is more in line with that of the depressive person than the normal. This was true for cartoon films as well as for the more unpleasant film. This depressive, emotional vision also is something covert, normally unexpressed. The person seeing films in free vision sees them as he would on the left hemisphere. In other words there is a secret hidden vision, speaking with an alternative emotional voice which is the depressive expression of the right hemisphere, but this is normally suppressed and overlaid so that it is not dominant in ordinary conduct. The question inevitably arises as to whether this depressive vision can struggle free of the forces which normally control it to cast the person into a depressive framework of perception and create a depressive illness, and what the circumstances and precipitating forces for this may be.

The idea that depression comes out of the right hemisphere and there is a specific part of the brain which produces depression raises many possibilities, not the least of which is that of warring factions in the different brain systems and that the part of the brain responsible for the production of depression may come to dominate the intellectual and emotional life of the patient to the extent of producing a pathological condition. The possibility arises not only that as scientists we shall eventually be able to map the mind onto the brain but also that we shall be able to map those illnesses which affect the mind back onto the brain and thus create a cartography of mental illness as it relates to the brain.

Schizophrenia

There are many examples of this neuropsychological approach to psychiatric illness. As the major example of psychiatric disturbance which can be interpreted in the light of a failure of the mechanisms of the brain, the patterning of which is revealed by neuropsychological methods, we quote the case of schizophrenia. The observations we report arose largely as an offshoot of the author's own investigations whilst observing patterns of information transmission in the normal human brain. Schizophrenia is the mental illness which is the largest of all causes of severe mental disablement. The cost to the community in terms of human suffering, as well as loss of employment and earnings, is very severe. It is a disorder which leads to a detachment from the world. The patient shows abnormal ways of thinking, and speech is disturbed. The disorder is based upon a severe programmed misconception of the world and a disconnection from it. It is a disease especially of youth. The steady deterioration of the personality usually shows itself in adolescence. The great majority of cases start at puberty or adolescence. It is estimated that two thirds of the cases occur between the fifteenth and thirtieth year. Many of the cases which show the disorder later may have in fact been developing it insidiously over a number of years.

In a typical form, schizophrenia consists of a slow, steady deterioration of personality. It involves the capacity for emotional expression, both the capacity to feel emotion and the capacity to express it. There is a progressive loss of feeling, the mood becoming shallow, "there is neither warmth in laughter nor depth in despair." Embarrassment may be caused by inappropriate behaviour on the part of the patient and he may adopt peculiar postures and grimaces. Disorders of conduct, thought, and an increasing withdrawal of interest from the environment are typical. He may, for example, be convinced that he is the victim of evil powers or that his thoughts are controlled by external forces. Voices may be heard which as hallucinations repeat his thoughts, make obscene comments, or threaten and abuse him. These may be so real to the sufferer that he talks back.

It is possible that in the future a clear physical picture of the disorder and its causes will emerge, although it is fair to say that it has not done so at the present time. Evidence indicating a physical basis has been gathered over a number of years. Heredity plays a part and there are also social disabilities associated with schizophrenia. It was reported that there was an arrest in the males of the ability to produce sperms. The weight of the heart may be reduced; the hormone balance is disturbed. Other reports show that there is an abnormal distribution of hair on the patient's body. There may be hair on the face in the females, scanty beard and horizontal hair distribution in males. Then again there are indications of biochemical abnormalities; a discussion of these is, however, beyond the scope of this book. Some of these disorders and unusual physical patterns can be attributed to the abnormal way of life of the individual, but taken together they provide strong indication of a physical basis to the disorder.

Symptoms of Schizophrenia

The main symptoms of schizophrenia are the following:

1. Disturbances of thought
2. Disturbances of emotion
3. Disturbances of volition
4. Catatonic symptoms
5. Primary delusions
6. Hallucinations

DISTURBANCE OF THOUGHT: The most characteristic single aspect of the thought disorder of schizophrenics is described as the "knight's move" in thought. This distinguishes the form of the thought disorder from that in other types of mental illness. Thought is typified by its disjointed uncoordinated aspect, never direct, always stepping slightly to one side. In early cases the thought disorder may appear as a "wooly vagueness" and an inconsequential following of side issues. The patient is led off course by one train of associations to another. This makes it very difficult to follow the meaning or train of associations, and indeed the patients themselves may consider that they are being very profound when in fact their speech appears to be vague and inconsequential to the listener. Also their thoughts may turn to philosophical and mystical subjects where words used have a special meaning to the patient but again confuse rather than assist the listener.

Yet another feature is known as "thought blocking." Here

the patient, as the name suggests, may quite suddenly interrupt the flow of ideas and be unable to continue with the discussion or argument along those lines. This appears to be essentially similar to the thought disturbance experienced by normal people when they are, for example, unable to recall a name or when under stress a person forgets quite suddenly and irrevocably the sequence of his argument. Another symptom is described as "pressure of thought." The patient now feels that a multitude of ideas are passing through his mind. He is unable to single out ideas, unable to think clearly—his mind is confused and chaotic.

DISTURBANCES OF EMOTION: "Emotional blunting" is the phrase used characteristically to describe this aspect of schizophrenic disorder. The person may at first show some incapacity for the experiencing of emotion. As time goes on the flattening of emotion continues and the patient responds less and less with his emotions in what we think of as the normal way. As a consequence of this the patient has an incapacity for emotional contact with others, a lack of "rapport." As a result the patient may seem cold and distant to others. Accompanying this lack of emotional response is something else which disturbs the relationship between the schizophrenic and those around him, a tendency to respond with emotions which are inappropriate to the situation. For example, a trifling affair may be treated with great seriousness—the patient bursts into tears at the fall of a raindrop from a leaf; he laughs when told of the death of a parent or a friend. This is known as the "incongruity of affect" and distinguished authors have described it as "a further example of the splitting of the personality."

DISTURBANCES OF VOLITION: Here again the most common disturbance is a blunting of willpower. The patient may himself complain about the weakening of his will. He falls into a life of inactivity, spending days in bed and failing to progress in his work. Such behaviour is related to autistic daydreaming. In addition to symptoms of this kind there may also be "negativism," for example, the peculiar gesture of half proferring and half withdrawing the hand in a handshake. Bleuler introduced the term "ambivalence" to apply to actions of this type and indeed to the whole field of the motivation of the schizophrenic.

CATATONIC SYMPTOMS: Stupor may on occasion be a symptom. The patient apparently withdraws into a world of delusional fantasies and many stuperose patients apparently experience nothing in that state. Abnormal behaviour is observed in severe states of catatonia where the patient may hold one fixed posture for considerable periods of time or show an abnormality whereby the limbs can be moulded and take up the postures into which they have been shaped.

PRIMARY DELUSIONS: In their purest form, delusions appear suddenly, fully developed and are immediately believed by the patient. They involve the process by which the patient interprets the world and are generally said to be symbolic in nature. "For example a young woman listened to the BBC News Bulletin, suddenly realized that the announcer was talking about her." This peculiar disturbance in the way the individual interprets the world is most easily seen in the early cases. The picture is obscured subsequently by secondary delusions and rationalisations, and of course once the patient has accepted the primary delusion as substantial and real then there may be no end to the subsequent development and elaboration of it.

HALLUCINATIONS: These are often a conspicuous sign of the illness and may easily be elicited. Auditory hallucinations may be the first sign of the beginning of a schizophrenic illness. They may appear only on a single occasion or they may appear throughout the illness, overwhelming and indeed directing the patient's conduct for much of the time. Auditory hallucinations may accompany each action with their comments, even, for example, repeating aloud what the patient is silently reading. In some cases they consist of whistling only or of inarticulate noise. Their "unreal" appearance, even if recognised, does not reduce the patient's belief in their reality. In fact, they are more than frequently accepted with utter conviction. Many patients localise the voices in the head, speak of thoughts coming aloud or of thought echo. Besides hallucinations of hearing, there are also those of touch, smell, and taste, as well as disturbances of body sensation. Patients may report, for example, that the flavour of food has been interfered with, or that gas has been let into the room by hostile people, or that certain parts of their skin are hot or cold or feel as though they have been sprayed with fine sand. Visual hallucinations, on the other hand, are rare but they do occur.

Current Views

There is great interest at the present time in the conditions described as the schizophrenias and explanations range from hypotheses of biochemical abnormality to social and philosophical interpretations on the grand scale.

Lying between these extremes are the modern interpretations relevant to a neuropsychological view. Most important of these perhaps is the view that disturbance of perception is one of the cardinal features of the disorder.

Perceptions of reality are disturbed and so investigations have focussed on the perceptual processes. The evidence, however, suggests that as far as the basic perceptual processes go, at least as measured by thresholds, these are more or less intact. There are, however, disorders at the higher levels of perception and this has been a source of much speculation. Estimates of size, distance, and time may be affected. There are also suggestions of gross defects of the process of attention. This suggests that if there is involvement of the processes of perception, it is the higher more cognitive capacities that show this defect, and that at the elementary level perceptual processes are essentially preserved.

Another similar view is that there is a deficit of activation. The acute patient is believed to suffer from an inability to restrict the range of attention, and is thus at the mercy of a variety of sense impressions from all parts of the environment. Chronic patients are believed, on the other hand, to be suffering from unusually high levels of activation with a consequent narrowing of attention—thus many external sensory items do not enter consciousness at all.

Another similar view commonly expressed in writings on

schizophrenia is that there exists a disordered process of inhibition. It is known that there are inhibitory processes at work in the internal fabric of the brain and these, it is assumed by the nature of the pathology, fail to function effectively. One view is that the patient shows behaviour which does not extinguish properly because of the abnormal processes of inhibition.

Another prevalent notion is that disorders of communication lie at the root of the problem.

The disorder is believed to be one principally of thought and language and this accounts for much of the disorder including the social difficulties the patient experiences.

The Split-Brain Symptoms

The term schizophrenia is derived from the Greek word "schizin" (to divide, to split) and "phren" (mind). Bleuler, the person who introduced the term, did so in a monograph which he published on this topic in 1911. According to Bleuler, the disorders of schizophrenia could be attributed to one morbid process which he describes as "the splitting of the personality." In other words, some parts of the mind were dissociated or disunited from others. Bleuler found the splitting within thinking itself. He thought that a loosening in the association of ideas was the primary and fundamental disturbance, and because the links are loosened in the chain of association, instinctual desires and unconscious wishes can intrude into the consciousness of the patient. The result is the disruption or distortion of his personality. Bleuler was on the search for a fundamental disturbance hoping that the symptoms could then be explained in terms of this one underlying process.

Some confusion arose in the use of the term schizophrenia, although the concept expressed by Bleuler held sway for a considerable time. Nowadays, it is fashionable to regard the symptoms as less of a "splitting" and more of a "disintegration" of the personality, or indeed not to talk of it in these terms at all. Lishman, for example, states that "the concept of 'split minds' implicit in the term 'schizophrenia' has always been something of an embarrassment to psychiatric terminology and has stimulated the eager imagination of lay people throughout this century." Although the conceptions of Bleuler may be regarded with a degree of disfavour, the concept of split-mind and the idea of splitting the personality suggested itself strongly to him as the result of his studies and the original formulation was a strong one.

Bleuler was not alone in his view, Stransky also emphasised the "splitting" of the psychological functions. He described a lack of coordination between emotions and thinking which is now generally accepted and referred to as the incongruity of affect.

The concept of the splitting of the personality was so obviously suggested to Bleuler by the nature of the material that we have to reexamine his concept and enquire if it was not then and is not now something valid. Is it the case that some parts of mental function can proceed in ignorance of other parts from which they have become dissociated? Are some parts of the mind dissociated from others? Will some aspects of mental ability run on in the absence of appropriate information to guide them? The question remains as to whether we cannot bring the dissecting microscope of neuropsychology to bear on the problems of schizophrenia to establish evidence of a functional splitting of the abilities so obviously implied in Bleuler's description of the disorder.

Schizophrenia can occur in association with organic disorders of the brain more than would be expected by chance and brain damage to the temporal lobes and the diencephalon has the most marked effect. We can also report evidence that the corpus callosum (the commissures between the two hemispheres) is involved in schizophrenia. This comes from studies recently reported in the *British Journal of Psychiatry* by Rosenthal and Bigelow. They took a variety of measures of different parts of the brain from autopsy patients. Ten who were not schizophrenic although suffering from other disorders and ten who were chronic schizophrenics. At the time of autopsy the brains were routinely cut and then examined. It was found that the schizophrenic patients showed an enlarged corpus callosum. This was significantly larger in the schizophrenic group, beyond the 0.001 level of significance. When the average corpus callosum width from all twenty brains were ranked in a descending order by size, the first nine measurements come from the schizophrenic specimens. It is interesting to note in this connection that the size of the corpus callosum did not correlate with any increase in weight. It should be remarked, however, that the sample was a small one in which to expect any relationship of this kind. It is clear that the observation of increased corpus callosum size in chronic "bad prognosis" patients raised many interesting possibilities, not least of those concerning subtle alterations of perception and the question of integration, and the possible disarticulation or mismatching between the hemispheres which such a condition may be expected to bring about.

It is clear from this study that a quite considerable enlargement of the corpus callosum comes about in chronic schizophrenia. It is not clear, however, whether this is the one underlying factor responsible for the morbid pathology or yet one more physical symptom of the illness. We are inclined to attribute much to this finding because the results of Rosenthal and Bigelow single out the corpus callosum as showing a change whereas other areas of the brain do not. Even so the question of what this implies about brain organisation and function still remains.

It is possible that enlargement of the corpus callosum occurs as a fortuitous result of the disorder and that in reality the patient has a hyperconnected brain which functions inefficiently because of the very multitude of connections between one side and the other. Studies of people born without a corpus callosum show that other parts of the brain become enlarged to compensate for its lack. It seems likely that the brain also works this way in schizophrenia and that enlargement of this area occurs in a desperate attempt by the brain to compensate for its inadequate functioning. This leads to the view that there is some fundamental failure to transmit information from one side of the brain to the other and this occupies a "central" position in the pathology and symptomatology of schizophrenia. In other words, the schizophrenic patient is a partially split-brain person and probably the rest of his brain is disconnected in other ways as well. If this is so then it should be possible to reveal something of this by showing that patients of this type do have difficulty in integrating information between the two "half-brains."

The classic method to show the nature of the link between the hemispheres is to get the subject to crossmatch two pictures flashed to the different visual half-fields from which they then project upwards to the hemispheres. The subject then has one picture at one hemisphere and another picture at the opposite hemisphere. His task is to indicate if the two pictures are the same or different.

Evidence of split-brain symptoms or partial disconnection came from an experiment conducted by the author in collaboration with a colleague, J. G. Beaumont. We flashed two digits at the same time, two shapes at the same time, or two numbers at the same time, one member of the pair to one hemisphere and the other member of the pair to the opposite hemisphere. People seeing the pictures were asked to state whether the two were the same or different and, of course, on some trials they were the same and on some different. The schizophrenic patients all suffering from an active illness were found to have difficulty in accomplishing this match between the hemispheres, whereas this same difficulty was not experienced by patients suffering from other kinds of psychiatric illness. The schizophrenic patients had no difficulty in identifying the pictures and they could also match, for the most part, when both pictures were flashed to the same hemisphere. The failure arose in matching between the hemispheres and it was this failure taken in conjunction with the evidence of abnormality of the corpus callosum which led us to suggest that split-brain symptoms may be characteristic of schizophrenia.

The question of the visual matching between the cerebral hemisphere is not the only one however. The case that disconnection operates in the brain would be immeasurably strengthened if it could be shown that, as in the split-brain patients, not only is there a visual disconnection but so also is there a disconnection between the activities of one hand and that of the other. This of course is a cardinal symptom of the split-brain condition and indeed is one of the distinguishing symptoms of corpus callosum pathology. The first point to note in the question of whether information of the functions of one hand may be available for incorporation in the programme of actions of the other concerns the very earliest onset of the capacity to bring the two hands together into a working relationship as occurs during the first month of infancy. Children at special risk to schizophrenia were studied by Fish and Hagin. It was found that one indicator of subsequent disturbance concerned precisely the ability to coordinate the two hands into coherent motor patterns. The disturbed children during the first year of life show a disability in bringing the two hands together in a coordinated response. This in fact cleared after the first year and during the second year of life the child behaved as normal; presumably restitution had been made. The point is clear, however, that there is an abnormality existing during the first year of life and employable as an indicator of a lack of hemisphere integration.

Adult schizophrenics performing manual work tasks also show something of these disorders of bimanual motor coordination. In investigations of motor skill where actions were studied by attaching lights to the limbs which were then photographed to build up a picture of the patient's movement, it was found that not only do the patients make many indecisive, jerky, and vacillating movements, thus dispensing with the idea that the patient performs poorly because he is slow, but that frequently the patient would prefer to use one hand in the performance of the task despite the fact that high levels of skill could only be achieved by the use of the two hands working together.

In addition to this, experiments conducted by Paul Green in conjunction with the present author show a degree of disconnection between the functions of the hands which is marked in extent. The patients were required to place their hands behind a screen and to perform a learning task with one hand, for example, to distinguish one of three boxes felt manually. If correct, the patient was touched on the hand to indicate the success of his activities. When the patient performed with one hand and was touched on only the same hand, in other words the patient received both the task and the reinforcement information to one and the same hand, learning proceeded perfectly well.

If, however, the patients were to perform with one hand and yet received the information which conveyed the correctness of his response to the other hand, then the patients experienced the greatest difficulty in the acquisition of the task and indeed many failed to learn at all. There is, therefore, a fundamental failure of intermanual transfer which seems to characterise schizophrenic disorder. This distinguishing split-brain symptom is indeed present and lends further weight to the view that some form of disconnection is present which has important effects upon behaviour in this condition.

There is also a disturbance of lateral balance. There may indeed be loss of function within the hemisphere itself, leading those components most clearly lateralised towards a decline. There are indications of an eroding of the patterns of language, something again which is more closely lateralised.

In our results we had an interest in the question of loss of function at one side of the brain or the other, specific to schizophrenia. Could a person have schizophrenia at one side of the brain and not at the other, for example? We did not find anything as dramatic as that. What we did find was a deficit specific to the hemisphere tested. On the right hemisphere the schizophrenic patient was deficient in matching letters one to the other. On the left hemisphere the schizophrenic patient was deficient in matching shapes one to the other and in matching numbers one to the other. We have found specialisms of each hemisphere in the normal brain to correspond to the deficits shown in schizophrenia. The brain is affected in its specialised abilities and these are no longer sharply differentiated. Not only are the two hemispheres partially disconnected by schizophrenia but the specialised capacities of each hemisphere are also eroded. It is possible that disconnection operates not only between the cerebral hemispheres themselves but also in some measure within the hemisphere to interfere with abilities concentrated in it.

Interpretation of the Symptoms

If brain disconnection exists as the result of schizophrenia then we may expect first that each hemisphere is to some degree disconnected from the other and that there will be a difficulty in integrating or articulating the products of the two hemispheres. Second, we may expect that some parts of function apparently run on without joining up or being governed by other parts thus producing bizarre effects in behaviour. It is difficult to single out any one symptom, any one cause as the basic factor, however the fact that the hemispheres are to some degree disconnected and that the patient appears as a partially split-brain person is evidence that the concept of brain disconnection is appropriate to the interpretation of this condition. The next course is to look for evidence supporting the basic principle in the rest of the symptomatology of the disorder.

Perhaps the most obvious examples are to be seen in the disturbances of emotion. Emotions become blunted and less finely tuned, but also they may run on out of step with the situation which normally releases them. In other words, the situation and the emotion run on parallel to each other but one is divorced from the other. The examples have already been quoted of the patient showing a lack of appropriate emotional response when told sad news and of tears and distress for inappropriate happenings. It seems therefore that in "incongruity of affect" the emotional activities are exercising their sway over the person but are doing so in a way in which information about the outside world and the appropriate controls and gearing are no longer able to operate. This suggests dissociation of cognitive and emotional spheres of the right and left hemispheres.

Something of this same concept can be applied to the creative life of the schizophrenic. Maps and plans, diagrams and drawings all with esoteric significance to the individual may be produced in abundance and yet these attempts make little if any sense even to the skilled observer. The creative product is divorced from the reality of the situation—the knowledge, the information which would guide the creative factions. Is it possible that the creative capacities of man can "run on" in some ungoverned and ungovernable way and that attempts at creativity represent the disturbed workings of a dissociated brain?

Obviously not all schizophrenic patients show these symptoms or show them clearly. The brain could be disconnected according to many different patterns and it may be that the pattern is not the same in each case. The problem of whether there may be disconnection types can be considered as a secondary thing, it is the principle of whether functional disconnection can be said to occur or not that is our concern at present. If the patient has a disconnected brain then it is clear that information about the world cannot be linked up with the centres of emotion. The dissociation between thinking and feeling is beyond doubt, and inevitably these aspects of function must take some independent course. The creative abilities appear to be divorced from an appropriate context and from information which might be used to guide them. There are other symptoms where a similar interpretation can be made. Take the case of "ambivalence," whereby different courses of action are embarked upon successively and the individual vacillates between them, for example, the gesture of half proferring and half withdrawing the hand. It should be pointed out that examples of this type of behaviour are not unknown in the split-brain cases, in the first case reported by Bogen and Vogel, the patient would untie his dressing gown cord with one hand and do it up again with the other, reach towards his wife with one hand and push her away with the other.

It is probably in the realm of hallucinations that the concept of disconnection comes most into its own. Whistling and inarticulate noises, the presence of echo, voices localised in the head are all symptoms which seem to relate in an obvious kind of way to impairment of the physical system of the brain. If the hemispheres are disarticulated then it would be expected that the information passing across is itself distorted, full of noise, and likely to be disruptive rather than enhancing the capacity for function on reaching the other side.

It is clear that we know very little about the way in which the body is commanded into action by the brain, however, it seems completely plausible that the means for action follow from a series of decisions taken at different levels. There is, so to speak, an orchestration of the brain which ultimately leads to action. In other words, there are many decisions—"many voices." The theory of disconnection would lead to the view that some parts of the orchestration become split from others, and so there are elements continuing independent paths uncoordinated with the rest. Possibly the patient as a result is compelled to respond to these aspects of mental life and it is this which creates so many difficulties for him. These dissociated elements could relate to thought disorder and the impoverishment of mental life.

Again if one follows the analogy of a breakdown of the orchestration of the functions of the brain because some parts are disconnected from others, it is possible to see that a lack of volition and will would follow as a consequence because different strands would occupy the final common path in the control of individual behaviour. It would also follow that the splitting of some parts of the orchestration from others would result in the breakdown of the division between internal and external reality and result in marked disturbances of thoughts.

Many of the disturbances so typical of schizophrenia are reflected in the products of speech. Language is somehow twisted, distorted, and disturbed and in its most florid form has the appearance of meaning and is believed by the patient to have meaning, yet to the clinician much of the speech may fail to make sense. In much schizophrenic speech, meaning can be discerned and there are those who believe that it is intelligible and understandable in its own context. It is worth noting at this point that a disturbance of speech, the production of inappropriate words or the speaking of what amounts to nonsense, will of itself have profound and far-reaching effects because it will immediately lable the person as "mad" in the popular concept and in one stroke act to cut him off and isolate him from society. The individual even with the assistance of a sympathetic family finds himself unable to communicate and indeed many of the other symptoms could follow secondarily from this one factor. With disturbed, uncontrolled, and paraphasic speech the individual finds himself at once in a hostile and unsympathetic world. The patient does not always and of necessity talk in a fragmented and disconnected way although permanent disturbances of this type are often a stable feature of the illness. The disturbances exist at a variety of different levels, ranging from substitution of some speech forms for others to complex expressions of pseudophilosophical wordiness. It may be that some language disturbance could be interpreted in the light of disconnection symptoms. If we were to think of a brain which is partially disconnected then we may expect that some forms of information would simply not be available to the speech system, in which case it would be expected that language would run on in an empty unguided fashion or that language would be distinguished by the poverty of its expression.

If raw and unprocessed information gets to the speech system—information which would not normally do so—again we may expect disturbances of speech. This time, however, the disturbances would be distinguished not by their poverty but by their florid, uncontrolled nature. If the normal route to the speech system breaks down then appropriate linguistic products may not arrive through the system whereas inappropriate ones may. The intrusion of irregulated content, not processed properly, unorganised in sequence, could indeed create a pressure upon the powers of linguistic expression as different strands of disorganised language compete for expression.

It will be clear that these ideas of brain disconnection as applied to schizophrenia are based on incomplete evidence. It will also be clear that the type of disconnection which appears to operate is not in the same mould or patterning as that seen in split-brain individuals. Nonetheless, some disconnection is apparent and the pattern by which it occurs remains to be systematically elaborated and worked upon. It may well be that in the fullness of time a disconnection syndrome can be identified for this disorder. The question will then have to be asked if this is still only one more symptom which we have uncovered of this baffling condition or does it represent the underlying morbid state causing the individual to show the behaviour that he does. Certainly the suggestion is that the concept of the "splitting of the personality" as an interpretation of the disorder, although currently unfashionable, may not be far from the truth and that as an interpretation it is one which receives support from the new facts of the recently discovered split-brain symptoms of this disorder.

Chapter IX

HIGHER MENTAL FUNCTIONS

Evolution of Higher Mental Processes

DURING the history of the brain the functions which it shows were not only shaped but originated in those processes which promoted the survival of the individual. That the brain of man evolved out of forms more primitive is a view which goes largely unchallenged and the fact is that the march of evolution has changed the brain step by step to increase the sophistication and the complexity of its organisation. The view that there has been a history of progressive change leading to ever greater sophistication has much to recommend it. It has been argued that evolutionary forces exerted an influence pervasive over all qualities of the brain—making the machinery that little bit more sophisticated, endowing the individual with a marginal increase in the success with which it interrelates with the environment, and providing that important extra premium increasing the very capacity to survive. This pervasive influence is something which stretched over all aspects of the work the brain was called on to perform. The touch of evolution fell upon the fixed and relatively unchanging components of the individual's behaviour, it fell upon mechanisms for the expression of basic instincts, but more than this it also fell upon the flexible and adjustable aspects of the individual's behaviour. It fell upon those aspects which cause the individual to respond not in a blind, impulsive way but which lead him to come to a higher relationship with the environment—the patterns of perception, the ability to store and retrieve significant information from memory, the ability to profit from experience, the ability to anticipate the future course of events, and most of all the ability to pursue a course of action determined by reason and logic. The forces of evolution act upon fixed patterns of action but they also act at

172

the very highest levels of mental life. There is in other words an evolutionary history of higher mental function associated with the emergence of intelligence.

Not only is it important to consider if the brain has proceeded upon an evolutionary course, but so also the question must arise as to whether there is a continuing evolution of intelligent behaviour and creative ability at the present day. Will the emergent intelligence of man reach still higher peaks of attainment and sophistication? Does the brain of man continue on its evolutionary course?

Julian Huxley expressed the view that the physical evolution of man was coming to a halt. For him the main physical forces were spent and for him evolution is to be expressed not through any further efficiency and sophistication of the brain but through an increased use of the equipment with which man is endowed to further the aims of his social and cultural progress. There is, in other words, a continuing evolution, but one of social thought and conduct which takes over where physical evolution leaves off.

Huxley based this view on what he regarded as an important fact—that the force of survival no longer operates as a significant feature in human existence. Man, given ordinary health, is able to survive in a protected environment and to reproduce his kind aided very substantially by the developments of modern medicine. The biological constraints are in the course of change, and limitation of family size through methods of contraception is a major force in society acting to reduce the pressure of numbers and the clamour for life space as some survive and others perish.

Against this argument it should be said that the world has not yet provided a hospitable home for all its citizens. Those primitive conditions which prevented the survival of many in the past still operate in communities today. Famines exist across the face of the world and there are signs that the food resources may not be as abundant as we had until recently believed. The fact is that there are many stages along the life course of the individual where survival can be threatened, and the traditional Darwinian concept that numbers are restricted by competition between species members or between different species may represent only one side of the coin.

Despite attempts by man himself at cushioning the environment for his own protection, the world is still in many respects a hostile one and a certain degree of resilience may be necessary simply to exist as a human being. A certain vitality is necessary, for example, for the infant to come through to full term and many potential human beings fail during this early part of the course. The infant after conception is endowed with life but it falters before reaching the outside world. Despite the advances in medicine there is a genetic selection on a major scale which still operates here. Although birth mortality has been reduced to low levels by the devoted care of obstetricians and gynaecologists, the infant also has to contend after birth with an environment in which hostility resides. The infant may fall prey to infection and infant mortality is still with us; it is still the case that many children do not reach adulthood because they lack the resilience to contend with the microbiological hostilities in some societies and the competition for the ecological resources of their environment in others.

We have pointed out that the survival factor is still strong in shaping the contemporary evolutionary course of man. If we should accept that the developments of modern medicine render this force no longer as powerful as in the past, we would still argue that evolution proceeds by virtue of mechanisms in which the question of survival plays only a limited or perhaps insignificant role. Here we have to confine the discussion of evolution to the development of intellectual function but naturally we deal with broad principles which could equally well operate in other areas of human function.

Where organisms are in a continuous fight for survival this will promote a rapid force for change likely to affect in some way or another all aspects of the individual's life and existence and this is, so to speak, evolution in top gear. Although evolution may not be in top gear this does not mean that there can be no lack of progress at a slower pace. If genetic material can be removed from the population, as fresh material is incorporated into it, then evolution can proceed. Genetic material can be removed from the population on a purely chance basis. When a species declines and ultimately becomes extinct its genes disappear. In the same way, genes equally could disappear on a purely chance basis and genetic material cease to exist in the population because of the random failure of individuals to mate and to produce offspring. Of course, the scarcer the gene becomes in the population the more likely it is that a gene will pass a threshold of no return and eventually reduce itself to zero.

The amount of genetic material that can be carried by the individual is limited. New members chosen for the football team inevitably displace the old, and if there is any creation at all of new genetic substance then this by its incorporation will be responsible for the exclusion of some of that which already existed. With progress and change there is an inevitable release of the grasp upon the old. Another factor is that there is clustering of the genetic material and if a gene should be linked in with a cluster but that gene was a "bad gene" in that it prevented the individual from living to produce offspring, then not only will the "bad gene" pass out of the population but it will also take with it the cluster to which it is linked and within which it is accommodated. Whole complexes of genes can thus be removed from the population at large by this process, not to reappear.

More important, however, than the question of how genes may diminish, go into a decline, and ultimately become reduced and extinguished, is the question of the creation of the new genes and incorporation of them as fresh genetic material. The gene system is exposed to a continuous shifting mutation and as new mutations occur evolution takes a step forward. If the mutation proves to be unfavourable the individual will not survive or may well be infertile. If favourable, then the fresh genetic material for the superior and advanced organisation of the brain will pass into the gene pool and become incorporated as part of the genetic stock of the race. The fact that man no longer needs to fight off adversaries with his bare hands does not stop this from happening—it is not the aggressive encounter but the hostile environment itself, including natural microbiological warfare, which acts against the survival of all except the strong. Favourable genetic mutations therefore still become incorporated whereas the less favourable pass out of being.

Is it the case that genetic mutations produce individuals with superior organisation of the brain who are in a position to make a unique contribution to our understanding or to the development of the world around us? If so, such abilities may convey no special advantage for survival in a stable and ordered society to the individuals possessing them and yet they are not disadvantageous to survival. If such abilities continue as a genetically based inheritance, the gifts of the individual will be incorporated into the genetic stock of the society and although not awakening a superior brain organisation for generations to come, nonetheless the potential exists crystallised and realisible in the genetic code. The nature of genius is such that given a superior organisation of the brain it may well flourish only as the result of a haphazard series of events in the life of the individual—the pursuit of a career path which allows reign to the individual's particular gifts and abilities, encouragement and enthusiasm during youth, the motivation to grasp a problem and work at it. Genetic gifts are by no means the sole requirement for becoming a genius.

It may be that radical rearrangements of the brain do confer advantages to the individual. In most cases, however, where there is gross brain abnormality such individuals are genetic freaks usually possessed of markedly inferior intelligence. The genetic processes can apparently only work within the framework of the structure of the brain as we know it to be and there is a limited canvas upon which it can work, although it must be said that gross structural reorganisation as a method of advance in the future is something which cannot be ruled out. Because inferior organisations of the brain frequently prevent survival or interfere with the sexual, cultural, and social mechanisms by which conception is brought about (thus inducing infertility) and superior organisations of the brain, whilst not necessarily promoting survival, do not inhibit it, it follows that the genetic processes which govern the workings of our brain are subject to continuous change.

The evolutionary processes have not stopped but continue actively in an upward direction. The brain according to this analysis is reaching out for higher and higher peaks of mental achievement. Although there may be an inexorable march upwards in the power of our mental processes through the action of evolution upon the brain, this does not at the same time refute the possibility of parallel cultural or social evolution or relieve man of the burden of taking hand in his own fate to ensure that those social and cultural changes which do take place are of the very finest quality.

Not only is there a potential for social and cultural evolution but man may even now, through the action of biological forces as they operate in the brain, be on the route to advanced forms of intelligence that will enable him to produce a proper order to human affairs. Succeeding generations may not only be more gifted but also in consequence be wiser in their conduct one towards the other.

If the brain continues to evolve as we have reason to believe it will, then we may speculate about the future course of higher mental development. Will it proceed by channels of thought unknown to us? Will new and totally different forms of mental action evolve? We cannot readily foresee the circumstances in which man may live or the environment he may create for himself, which could result from or lead to major evolutionary changes of the brain. Rational speculation can be made about the future course of evolution based upon those tendencies which already operate to provide the brain with its special and unique qualities and which already point to changes in certain directions.

Learning and the Brain

We have seen that one feature which distinguishes the mind of man is not only the multiplicity of forms which mental activities can take, but also the fact that higher mental activities are instrumental in promoting a manipulation of the environment. Higher mental processes in this sense are something essentially adaptive—used by the individual to establish a working relationship with that individual's environment and in this sense they are essentially flexible—and something which promote and greatly facilitate the life-style of the individual. The action of higher mental processes in allowing adaptability, adjustment, and flexibility should be thought of not just in the context of the physical world but also in the social setting, where this very adaptability has allowed man not only to accommodate but also to create the widely diverse cultural patterns of social organisation that we see in the world today. Whatever the evolutionary route by which the capacity for flexible rearrangement emerged and however this was shaped in the past, it is the case that this attribute represents a significant step in human evolution and as such it is a distinguishing and almost defining characteristic of the mental makeup of man.

There is a long history of the use of adaptive response and indeed the very origins of nervous system control may well lie in the need that organisms have to adapt. There is an amazing plasticity particularly in the early life of the organism. There is a plasticity not only of regions but also of the very cell units themselves. Although organising principles govern and shape the formation of the brain the fact is that despite these, it is an organ still capable of great flexibility. Although the brain bends to the force of the overall organising principle, at the same time the vast fabric of the brain becomes committed only slowly to the performance of discrete functions and there is considerable indeterminancy so that the various parts of the brain are capable potentially of subsuming numerous different functions.

It happens, however, that with the progress of the individual through life, parts of the brain do take up a defined function and they do fall into a set mould. The pattern of their action becomes determined for them. This pattern of commitment is most usually thought of within the context of physical development. Cells take up a particular function and because of this they become incorporated within the physical working entity of the brain. It is equally clear however that commitment of the brain need not be thought of exclusively within the context of physical organisation.

Modern research shows that the brain can also be shaped, moulded, and committed by the nature of the experience which the individual receives. This passes into the brain acting to transform the nature of the substance of which the brain is composed. For example, the cells of the visual cortex of animals exposed to vertically striped patterns respond differently than the cells of the cortex of the brain of animals exposed to horizontally striped patterns. There is a principle of response by exposure learning which shapes up the brain to become what it is and it is this which enables the brain to come to some fundamental adjustment with the environment. The capacity to respond and to adjust to the environment can be regarded as one of the primary advantages of a sensitive brain and nervous system shaped by the process of evolution.

It is clear that the brain by virtue of changes in its physical structure is registering the events which impinge upon it and that these actually change the brain into the thing that it is. In the way in which early experiences act upon the brain we have a model of fundamental importance for understanding the learning process. Out of this initial plasticity and then later commitment we have the first origins of learning and of the higher apprehensive processes which have developed to such an extraordinary degree of sophistication in man. We could see the commitment of cells to the registration of the environment as the fundamental means by which learning comes about and the thing which the cell is committed to as the basis of the process of memory.

Whether cells get held in reserve for subsequent commitment throughout the life of the organism in order to preserve the sustained flow of learning is difficult to say. There is evidence of a decline in learning capacity as man matures but it may be that cells are not always permanently committed and if a small number could, after the passage of time, break free of the commitment which they have then this in turn allows for fresh registration of the events of the environment and some recommitment to take place.

Another feature of the human brain relevant to the question

of learning and remembering is that of restitution of function. This is the tendency of the brain to reorganise its action in the face of damage, to minimise the effects which damage may have, and to·restore as much function as is possible. After a gross insult to the brain the patient may be seriously debilitated but after a time he makes what adjustment is possible and often compensation for the damage proceeds to such an extent that it may be impossible to tell that the brain had sustained damage at all. Clearly the brain comes to some fresh organisation of its function after damage has been sustained and the power of the brain to reorder its functions in this way is indeed one of its most remarkable features. Exactly how the brain achieves this is not known but in most cases not only is there a resynthesis and restructuring of that which the patient has lost through the action of the rest of the brain, but also in the case of intellectual functions there may be some fresh synthesis including the coming together of what remains to obviate and cancel out the deficit resulting from the loss of the destroyed tissue. The capacity of the brain to sustain damage and yet to come to a reordering of its function once again illustrates the cardinal feature of flexibility and capacity for adaptation to changing circumstances. The physical structure of the brain is something which not only carries a principle of overall organisation but the substance of the brain takes up, reflects, and mirrors the tasks which it is called on to perform and it is here that the force of events acts upon the brain to shape it the way that it is.

We may regard the capacity of the sense organ to etch out its trace upon the brain as absolutely fundamental in that an organism that fails to register events will fail to learn. Yet at the same time it is clear that there is a more active principle involved. Why is it that we learn some things and not others? Why is there this impulse towards motivated acquisition? Whatever the nature of the discussion with regard to registration or active search in learning, the capacity to learn represents one of the fundamental activities comprising man's higher mental functions. When we consider the nature of learning as it relates to the brain we have to consider not only the question of commitment but also that of restitution of function. Evidence leads to the view that the capacity to be shaped by experience may well be a fundamental property of living nervous tissue. At present neuropsychologists may be reluctant to single out isolated parts of the brain uniquely responsible for learning, although with regard to specific habits or discretely learned actions it may well be that specific parts of the brain are involved.

Creativity and Consciousness

It has to be remembered that the human brain is capable of a vast array of activity, some of which is of a very specialised nature, some of which is rather more pervasive. Most striking of the abilities which we think of as specifically, if not exclusively, human are those for rational thought and incisive action, in fact the ability to find logical and rational solutions to the problems which face us in everyday life. There is even more in the nature of human ability than merely acting as a logical machine. There are, for example, the great creative realms of conduct where man explores not only his own universe but also the realms of his own mind. This is a pursuit which taxes the limits of human accomplishment and yet all the same it is the possession of these abilities which is likely to change the face of human conduct.

Whilst neuropsychology has undoubtedly been successful in relating psychological function to the action of the brain in a precise delimited way, or indeed in respect to the larger sphere, it is when we come to consider creative abilities beyond that of mere intelligence that our knowledge stops short and the attempt to relate what we do know about creative action breaks down. We, therefore, have to accept the limitations of our knowledge. Often the advances of neuropsychology have been dependent upon gaining knowledge of the workings of the brain, but probably in this instance something approaching an answer can only come when there is a solution at the psychological level to the question of what is creative ability? How can we measure it and how can we know what it is?

Although the neuropsychologist has at present little to say about the large scale topics of creative endeavour and about the nature of originality, at the same time we should not be discouraged by these deficiencies. We may regard the situation as one which hinges almost exclusively on the question of the development of suitable ways of measuring creativity and originality. Already brave attempts have been made in respect to this and it is only a matter of time before use of techniques to investigate the essential creativity and originality of the mental makeup of man can be used in conjunction with neurosurgical and other approaches to indicate something of the underlying brain organisation which is capable of bringing creativity and originality about. Just as Lashley was able to organise his studies out of an almost total ignorance of how the brain can conduct the processes of learning and with a few sufficient techniques which revealed the nature of learning, so with the development of techniques for the study of creative behaviour and originality is likely to emerge an understanding of the fundamental control mechanisms of the brain in the genesis of this essential quality which is a distinguishing feature of the human brain.

William James says that consciousness is what you might expect in a nervous system which has become too large to steer itself. For William James, consciousness could be regarded as an emergent which results from the complexity of the brain as it is. Others held that there was something more pervasive than this, Sherrington for example states, "Do we not think of this 'I' as a cause within our body. Our perception seems to look out from our body. The body seems a zone immediately about that central core." The fact is that the term consciousness has been employed to mean so many different things that if we ask the question "How does consciousness relate to the action of the brain?" we must be prepared to examine not one but a variety of different things and to pursue the discussion at a much more detailed level.

One view is that consciousness is the product of the mechanisms for sleep and wakefulness. This topic has already received some discussion in Chapter III. This type of consciousness, it is held, relates to the workings of mechanisms outside of the cerebral cortex. Penfield thought that although all regions of the brain may be involved in normal conscious processes, the indispensable substrates lie outside the cerebral cortex, probably in the higher brain stem. As evidence of this, Penfield put forward the view that large areas of the cortex can be removed without loss of consciousness but, on the other hand, consciousness is invariably lost when the function of the higher brain stem is interrupted by injury. Consciousness was never the same thing; it was a stream, a changing phenomenon, flowing onwards except during sleep and coma.

A consideration of sleep and wakefulness could lead to the view that there are particular regions of the brain to be nominated as consciousness centres. This, it is argued, is demonstrated by the undoubted fact that the patient with damage in these regions does pass into a state of coma or permanent sleep. It may be thought on the basis of cases such as these, that the question of whether the whole brain takes part in consciousness or only localised regions are involved has been settled in favour of the latter view. Penfield did not, in fact, think this, as will be evident from the statement of his view, yet at the same time there is an obvious case to be made for the more direct expression of this standpoint.

There are two points to be made about the brain stem participation in conscious processes. The first is that the integrity of the brain stem, whilst something essential to the full expression of the flowing of consciousness, is at the same time not the seat of those conscious processes themselves. In other words, the integrity of the centres of wakefulness of the brain stem is a defining condition that there should be a full, alert, and vivid expression of the substance of consciousness. Yet even this view may have to be qualified by the second point to be made— that sleep may not always be a state which defines that a lack of consciousness shall occur, when the other attributes of consciousness are to be considered. Although the individual may have passed into a state of deep and profound sleep that person at the same time may be aware of a running panorama of events passing before him, events experienced with clarity and recalled with great certainty on occasions, the realm of his dreams experienced with the feeling of reality and yet experienced at the time when the individual is asleep and judged by what we know about the brain stem function to be in a state of unconsciousness.

Despite the puzzling example of the capacity to dream, it seems probable that the action of the midbrain is something which promotes the conditions for consciousness even if this relates only to the ability to exercise control over volitional movements through mental plans for action. As one needs a voice to speak, one needs a brain stem to be completely conscious, but this is only one step on the way, one of the defining conditions but not the whole of this complex thing. The conclusion which we reach is that the centre of wakefulness is not the centre of consciousness but merely an attendant thing or a defining condition.

Another view implicit in much thought about the process of consciousness is to regard it as something inextricably bound to language. The argument runs that words are essential to thought and that the fabric of our mental life is a verbal one based upon our knowledge of language. The fish that gets hooked and lifted out of the water sees that there is a fisherman in addition to the hook. The hook is an expression of the fisherman, an instrument of his desires. The baited hook may be all that the fish at first sees but subsequently when the fisherman is encountered even the fish could not be forgiven for thinking that the baited hook and the fisherman were one and the same thing.

Language is not the substance of mental action but an expression or an instrument of it. The person riding a bicycle, for example, does not need to translate all the actions of his limbs from some masterplan conceived in words. The great realms of artistic experience, music and painting, the visual arts, are not appreciated only by virtue of the fact that we can describe what we see or what we hear in words. Language is the handmaiden of consciousness and not the essential fabric or thing of which it is composed. Obviously we cannot seek the comprehensive description of the nature of consciousness processes by pointing to language as the only essential principle. There is more to consciousness than this.

The possibility that consciousness may express itself in forms other than those involving the linguistic code is seen most forcibly in the split-brain cases described in Chapter V. The idea has been put forward and forcibly argued that the split-brain patient possesses two potentially separate "streams of conscious awareness," virtually two separate "minds" within the single brain. The evidence for this is the apparent doubling where many fundamental aspects of consciousness are concerned. Each hemisphere can be shown to be responsive separately to stimuli, to perceive, to attend, to remember, and to learn. Each is capable to at least some degree of manipulating concepts of discrimination and of what may be broadly termed comprehension. All of this is obvious where the dominant hemisphere is concerned but it is also clear for the minor hemisphere which can make intermodal associations—concentrate on a problem, make generalisations, and mental associations among words. All of this it can apparently do outside the cognitive awareness of the dominant hemisphere.

Although it can be argued that there can be no evidence of consciousness in the minor hemisphere because there can be no report of a subjective state, and it is true that there can be no verbal introspective report from the minor hemisphere, nonetheless the minor hemisphere can indicate its state and can communicate. It cannot be said to lack consciousness by this criterion. Independent of the definition of consciousness is the fact that complex, continuing mental processes can occur in the minor hemisphere without being accessible to the mechanisms of introspection and verbal report—this means not that there is no consciousness but that the latter has been overemphasised as a criteria of consciousness in the past. Bogen (1969) has drawn together evidence for what he calls appositional functions in the nondominant hemisphere similar to what Freud called primary process thinking, something carried out more through pictorial concrete images than by the use of words.

The evidence that the minor hemisphere may after commissurotomy display a "will" of its own is somewhat anecdotal and best quoted from Sperry (1966). "While the patient was dressing and trying to pull on his trousers the left hand might start to work against the right to pull them down on that side. Or the left hand after just helping to tie the belt of his robe, might go ahead on its own to untie the completed knot, whereupon the right hand would have to supervene again to retie it. The patient and his wife used to refer to the 'sinister left hand' that sometimes used to push his wife away aggressively at the same time that the hemisphere of the right hand was trying to get her to come and help with something." Akelaitis described a rather similar phenomenon. One patient had a three week spell in which the hands would sometimes work in opposition on simple tasks. Another had difficulties when, for example, he would walk to the cellar he would be unable to advance over the threshold and would walk backwards and forwards for several minutes. There is further evidence which can be quoted from Sperry that the right hemisphere has a will of its own. "When it was apparent from his facial expression that he knew the right hand had performed incorrectly, the left hand folded behind him and sometimes restrained by the experimenter would make spontaneous movements as if to reach out and correct the error. When free use of both hands was permitted the patient usually was unable to arrange the blocks and/or pictures correctly, mainly because the right hand would always try to help and would consistently undo the superior accomplishment of the left."

Evidence about minor hemisphere accomplishment in the domain of will is even now somewhat equivocal because the evidence rests on the manifestation of motor action, and although the evidence does point to a distinct cognitive and volitional system it may still be that automatisms of the right hemisphere express themselves to create conflict in those instances we have described. Sperry was convinced, however, that surgery had left these people with two separate minds—two separate spheres of consciousness—but there were no complaints about split-consciousness and when both hands and both fields of vision were free to play their part, the patient gave no sign of feeling they were separately experienced or controlled.

Much has been built upon the fact that man has a unitary and undivided experience. The experience of mental unity remains intact despite extensive destruction of the cerebral hemispheres and it remained intact as judged by the split-brain evidence, although in the absence of language from the minor hemisphere to describe the nature of visual experience at that side it is probably impossible to say if a parallel and undivided visual experience exists at that side separate and independent to itself.

Eccles (1966) has given consideration to the question of free will in relation to the two separated hemispheres. He regards the dominant hemisphere as demonstrating the situation as it exists in the normal subject but he regards the conscious subject as having no control over what the left hand is doing. He regards the goings on of the minor hemisphere as never coming into the conscious experience of the subject. However who is the subject? The side of the brain that can speak? We could equally well deny consciousness to a person who is deaf and dumb if we suppose that the essence of being a person is to be hung upon the question of the carrying of consciousness by language. We have seen that the person who cannot speak need not be denied a stream of consciousness if that person can demonstrate comprehension and understanding, as can the nondominant hemisphere through means other than speech.

It is certainly possible to take the opposite view from Eccles and to suppose that each hemisphere of the human brain in the split-brain condition is in fact in receipt of all that we think of as characterising the conscious state of man, with the exception of the capacity to speak and the facility to describe in words the nature of the mental experience which takes place. Eccles based his view largely on the standpoint that there is a unitary experience of consciousness and that despite extensive damage to the brain this can proceed undivided. Yet we have to ask what it means to say that we have a unitary experience and what the significance of this can be. One approach to the problem of consciousness is that neural activity sets a chain of events into operation whereby the electrical activity evoked by sensory stimuli is steadily transformed through successively interconnected series of neurons.

Libet and Jasper describe the effects of applying very weak electrical pulses to the exposed cortex of conscious and anaesthetised patients with a view to determining the minimal stimulus required for a conscious experience. In the conscious subject there are small afterwaves and a delay of at least half a second intervenes before any sensation is experienced. This would correspond to a relay of about 200 synapses. Wilst the brain is actively at work there is never awareness of the multitude of processes through which it passes in order to achieve its total function.

We are aware of the movement of the hand around the clock face but never of the action of escapement upon cog or the action of one cog mechanism upon another. The stream of conscious perception is the final resolution or the surfacing of the processes which pass through the brain. What we perceive is itself compounded of a long chain of neural events about which we have no awareness at all. Stations and substations of the brain become called into action along the route. We should not confuse the fact that conscious perception is the emergent or final product with the view that it is a unitary thing or with the view that conscious perception takes place in only one sweep, for clearly it does not.

The television picture is compounded of a multitude of processes and yet the final product is something with a unitary aspect. The view that conscious perception emerges into awareness as the end result of a complicated chain of processes over which we have no awareness at all suggests, as was proposed by Freud, that consciousness itself, although important, may represent a small part of the work which the brain accomplishes. The vast mass of the work, in all probability not concerned directly with thrusting material into conscious awareness, takes up its position in the early part of the chain which ultimately leads to awareness, and thus its action is not likely to have the spotlight of conscious awareness ever cast upon it.

We have argued that the term consciousness has been employed often as though there is some one thing which by its very nature it must be, and yet the tendency has been to seize upon some aspect to the exclusion of others and at the expense of the recognition of the fact that under the umbrella of the term there are many actions at work. In fact, taken at large the term higher mental processes is itself not widely different in extent and scope from that which is usually meant by consciousness, except for an additional tone of awareness—the self looking at the self at work.

We have already pointed out that we need to be careful not to interpret the limiting constraints upon consciousness as consciousness itself. To hear a telephone conversation, the telephone must be in working order. The telephone is not the source of the telephone conversation but the instrument of it and is essential only insofar as an instrument is necessary. Similarly, it is important not to confuse the instrument of consciousness with that thing itself. Bearing these cautions in mind, we need to examine consciousness in a little more detail to differentiate those aspects which could be said to fall within its framework from those which do not.

In the first instance, we would have to single out awareness of the world—the flowing panorama of events and happenings which passes before us. Secondly, we may regard the capacity to store memories of part of the stream of events as an essential prerequisite for consciousness. Thirdly, there exists the capacity to manipulate and to reflect upon happenings which pass before us. Fourthly, there is an important working out of plans and projects for the future as well as the realisation of solutions to present problems. Finally, there is the volitional contract for patterns of action, the programming of the body to respond to the wishes and the intentions of the individual. In addition, all this may be accompanied by an extra awareness or a secondary insight of the individual at work. It follows that the sustaining principle of consciousness is no single thing and that attempts to relate consciousness to the workings of the brain in the search for a simple correlation may even now be premature. Investigation can proceed, however, by a much closer definition and a concerted effort within the framework of that to tie aspects of brain function to the essential steps along the way of man's conscious expression.

Some Major Clinical Syndromes

Much of modern neuropsychology has developed from work in the clinic—the natural laboratory where study is made of damage to the brain occurring as the result of disease or unfortunate accident. We deal here, therefore, not only with a science as a collection of modern knowledge of how the brain works but also as a medical discipline playing an increasingly significant role in the diagnosis, treatment, and rehabilitation of the person with a damaged brain. The practitioner of neuropsychology has to come to his subject with a good grasp of some of the essential concepts and terms used to describe the behaviour of people with a damaged brain. To facilitate this we review and describe some of the major syndromes seen in the clinic in association with damage to the cortex and explain something of the technical vocabulary used in the diagnosis and treatment of such cases.

Aphasia

One of the most common disorders encountered in the clinic is that of "aphasia" which broadly means a disorder of speech, language, and communication. The brother of Mrs. Sarah Siddons the great tragedian, John Philip Kemble, was said to have given a performance on the stage which might well be described as aphasic. He was a failed priest turned actor who had a rather formal style of playing (Leigh Hunt in *Dramatic Essays* edited by William Archer). "Kemble turned his head so slowly that people might have imagined he had a stiff neck, while his words followed so slowly that he might have been reckoning how many words he had got by heart."

Yet another example of a kind of aphasia was that reported in the *Thespian Directory* a contemporary biography of eighteenth-century actors and actresses which describes a Mr. Burton. "He joined Mr. Strickland's company at Market Street, Herts, where he appeared for the first time in the character of

David (Rivals) . . . we say appeared for though extremely per-
fect in his parts, fright had prevented all utterance, and his
brother performers, anticipating the meaning of his motions,
were obliged to declare to the audience what they knew he
intended to say."

If one talks about a disorder of language and communication
it soon becomes evident that this can mean several different
things. The patient, like Mr. Burton, may not be able to talk at
all. All speech ceases to issue from his mouth, this is known as
a condition of *mutism*. At the other extreme the patient may be
extremely fluent but what he says fails to make sense. He produces *jargon* without meaning. When we talk of aphasia, therefore, we group all these language disorders together under the
common term.

Another aspect of aphasia is that it can be caused by different
things. For example, the person who cannot speak is born
dumb and, despite the view prevalent in the fourteenth century
that "Dumb men get no lands," it is perfectly possible to be
deprived of the voice, to retain the intellect, and to hear and
understand language perfectly well. This happens where the
person has lost the voice. Equally where damage has destroyed
the part of the brain controlling the voice a kind of "dumb-
ness" that we call "aphasia" can be produced which deprives
the person of the ability to speak but leaves his understanding
and hearing of spoken language intact.

On the other hand, the person who is born deaf and dumb is
usually born deaf but never speaks because he or she cannot
hear the sounds of speech. It is in other words a hearing difficulty. The same holds with aphasia, for when the part of the
brain which interprets what people say to us and allow us to
understand speech is destroyed, then the aphasia is like that of
the deaf and dumb person where hearing is basically at fault
and the speech failure results from this. There are, therefore,
several causes of aphasia and it is necessary to look at these in a
little more detail.

MOTOR APHASIA: The first type of aphasia is that where the
patient develops a disorder of the speech apparatus—not the
voice itself but the part of the brain controlling the voice. Paul

Broca over a hundred years ago described the case of a fifty-one-year-old man who could understand perfectly what was said to him but could not perform when he himself was required to speak. After this patient died it was found that there was damage at the left hemisphere of the brain. An area of the cortex had been destroyed towards the back part of the frontal lobe (posterior part of third frontal convolution). There may not be a total loss of speech following damage to the speech motor system, instead the patient may show mild stammering or changes in the use of grammar in speech.

SENSORY APHASIA: When the part of the brain responsible for listening to speech and analysing it is destroyed the picture of loss is quite different. Basically the patient loses the power to understand speech including what he says himself. He speaks very fluently usually but he makes lots of mistakes in what he says. One patient, for example, when asked how he felt stated, "I felt worse because I can no longer keep in my mind from the mind of minds to keep me from my mind and up to the ear which can be to find among ourselves" (Kreindler, Calavrezo, and Mihăilescu in *Revue Roumaine de Neurologie, 8,* 1971). Another patient says, "Then he graf, so I'll graf, I'm giving ink, no gefergen in pane, I can't grasp I haven't grab the grabben. I'm going to the glimmeril let me go" (Brown in *American Handbook of Psychiatry,* vol. 4, edited by Arieti, 1975).

Patients develop this kind of disorder when a region of the brain known as Wernicke's area is destroyed. This lies further back in the brain than Broca's area and it lies at the top and back part of the temporal lobe (posterior part of the superior temporal convolution).

CONDUCTION APHASIA: When the areas between the two systems are destroyed a similar kind of aphasia is produced known as "conduction aphasia." The system for speech (motor system) is preserved and this acts fluently to provide a running stream of language, but the speaking system is cut off or disconnected from the hearing system with the result that the speaking part of the brain does not understand what it says and so it rambles, producing nothing more than fluent jargon. It may be, however, that the idea of a disconnection between one part of the brain and another, whilst substantially correct, is in reality too simple an explanation and that a destruction of a mechanism for language lying between the motor and the sensory system is in reality involved.

TRANSCORTICAL APHASIA: Speech and language of course can be affected by many gross disorders as they affect the brain. Where widespread damage exists the patient may be left with little more than the capacity for the compulsive repetition of empty phrases, echolalia. This type of aphasia involves many different types of failure at several levels and is usually the result of a decay process in the brain.

Recent Discoveries

We have described the classic speech areas of the brain at the speech hemisphere, usually the left. Recent studies show that the other hemisphere in split-brain man also has a level of vocabulary and understanding which is not insubstantial. The regions of the brain involved also stretch back to include a much wider area at the back of the brain than had formerly been supposed; substantial evidence is now accumulating that a part below the cortex—the thalamus—is also involved in producing language.

Apraxia

To the person who suffers from it apraxia presents a problem similar to that of Margaret Truman, daughter of the former president of the United States Harry S. Truman. When Margaret Truman gave a recital in Washington, Paul Hume the music critic of the Washington Post wrote the following notice. "Miss Truman is a unique American Phenomenon with a pleasant voice of little size and fair quality. . . yet Miss Truman cannot sing very well. She is flat a good deal of the time. . . she communicates almost nothing of the music she presents . . . There are few moments during her recital when one can relax and feel confident that she will make her goal which is the end of the song."

In apraxia there are few moments where one can feel confident that the patient will reach his goal—the successful completion of an act. Apraxia involves a loss of those everyday skills by which we carry out the normal planned sequence of our movements. If, for example, the patient is asked to touch his nose, he may think for a while, vacillate, and perhaps touch the top of his head. If he is asked to light a cigarette he may place the box of matches in his mouth and leave the cigarette on the table. If asked to complete items on the practical section of an intelligence test he may vacillate in his movements, show a total inability, or give up the test, often in tears. He has lost the power to carry out specific acts. At the same time with one part of his brain he remembers perfectly well what he is supposed to do, and usually if asked about it will say what that is and yet there is an utter failure when it comes to putting those commands into action. One part of the brain knows that he is failing and the patient becomes distressed, yet another part of the brain remains incapable of carrying out the action.

In typical cases, such as the one we have described, there is a failure to connect the idea of doing something with the actual doing of it. The patient knows perfectly well what he is supposed to do and yet remains unable to produce the correct action. This condition is known as *ideomotor apraxia*. Another aspect of apraxia sometimes distinguished and singled out is that of *apraxia for dressing*. This is a very obvious symptom when it occurs and here the patient loses the ability to put his clothes on in the correct order. He cannot remember how to get his legs into his trousers. He may put them on back to front. He may try to put a coat on before a shirt and the order of dressing is completely disturbed.

Another category is *constructional apraxia*. This is a more subtle defect which involves the loss of skills usually carried out by the hands and which have been acquired over a long period of practice and experience. If, for example, the patient is required to copy a design, he may completely fail to do so. If he is asked to copy a construction made from the blocks used on an intelligence test, then similarly he will fail to do so. The evidence shows that apraxia occurs with damage to the parietal lobes of the brain. There is evidence to suggest that some forms of apraxia are more closely linked to right hemisphere lesions than to those of the left hemisphere.

Amnesia

Many of us suffer from lapses of memory during ordinary life but where these become frequent or a large part of the patient's memory is missing, this is a clinical condition known as *amnesia*. That this is a severely disabling disorder can be seen from our own experience of forgetting at some crucial moment the name of a person who has to be introduced to someone else, and try as we will that name cannot be made available to us. The person to whom this happens frequently or characteristically and as something which touches upon all aspects of his life is at a very serious disadvantage indeed. Equally so the person who has received a blow on the head which obliterated all memory for a time previous to that blow is at a disadvantage. One colleague of the author received a blow on the head during a car accident and was subsequently prosecuted for dangerous driving. The blow not only knocked him out and gave him a concussion but subsequently he was unable to recall anything of the accident or the events leading up to it and there was nothing in his memory that he could draw on to help his own defence.

Perhaps the most impressive type of amnesia is that of the post-traumatic condition where, as in the case we have mentioned, the patient receives a blow to the head and his memory is subsequently seriously affected. *Post-traumatic amnesia* usually involves a loss of memory in which a complete slice of the patient's life experience is removed from him and he is no longer able to enter and explore in his mind that realm of experience particular to him.

After head injuries, infective disorders of the brain, or surgery on specific areas the state of *anterograde amnesia* develops. Here the patient has a disorder of memory after the event. The person involved in an accident may, for example, not only lose memory of the events surrounding the accident in which he himself is involved, but less commonly he may lose memories of events occurring some considerable time after the accident.

Disorders of memory can exist as the result of some upset of the process for storing memories. Sometimes the patient may be left not so much with a loss of individual memories of the events for that time but more with a defect of the mechanism by which new learning occurs. Patients fail to store their memories of current events and they may pass into a confused state where the world around them is interpreted in the light of those memories which they have preserved, which could be those of twenty years ago rather than those of the present day.

Another type of disorder is known as *retrograde amnesia*. Long after the person has recovered from the effects of a head injury there may exist a gap in memory for all events occurring before the accident. The crucial feature of this type of disorder is that it is a loss of memory of events before some critical incident such as a blow to the head. The extent of this amnesia may at first be quite considerable, stretching over weeks or even months, but with recovery it shrinks to span only a shorter time, most often less than a day in duration, but there may be a total loss of memory for that more restricted period.

In addition to these specific types of memory loss there are gross deteriorations in memory associated with diffuse pathology of the brain. The chief memory systems of the brain appear to involve subcortical components as well as those at the cortex. The subcortical areas are the hippocampus, the mammillary bodies, and parts of the thalamus. The cortical contribution is largely centred in the temporal lobe although other parts of the cortex are also involved.

Chapter X

PSYCHOTECHNOLOGY

THE emphasis of much recent research in psychology has been placed firmly on the study of those techniques by which behaviour can be manipulated and changed for the solution of essentially practical problems. This has been true in regard to the treatment of clinical disorders as well as in the much wider sphere of social, industrial, and educational enquiry where psychology can be seen as providing an armoury of techniques and methods to be put into use as occasion demands. This manipulation of behaviour through the use of technological skill has come to be called *psychotechnology*. We discuss here a particular area of psychotechnology where behaviour is modified and changed by direct or indirect interference with the physical processes of the brain. We are concerned with the technology of the brain and with the technology of behavioural control. In this chapter we focus on one of the most striking of modern developments, the use of neuropsychology for the purpose of solving some of the practical problems with which mankind is confronted.

It is well to be modest at this stage and to say that although there are striking benefits which psychotechnology can bring it is the case that some of the developments of this exciting discipline are as yet little more than a projection forwards to the future, and in the broad context much of what we think of as psychotechnology is little more than a plan for the development of the subject.

We have not yet seen the full flowering of this area but it is probably fair to say that it is poised on the brink of major development. Experimental forays have achieved success sufficient to validate the nature of our enquiry and large-scale application as a branch of medicine is the next thing. We have therefore to consider something of what the general application of such techniques may eventually mean. Some developments are rooted firmly in fact and it is these that we may rely upon to convey the full flavour of the approach to the control of behaviour through the psychotechnology of the brain.

Schwitzgebel and Schwitzgebel (1973) in their book *Psychotechnology: Electronic Control of Mind and Behaviour* make the point that technology is here to stay. They illustrate this by specifying the record player as a technological advance which provides communication with millions of individuals, communication through the senses and into the brain. Communication, furthermore, which has benefited man enormously and provided him with a great source of the finest pleasure. Technology need not all be bad as this example testifies. Our purpose at the present time is not however to weigh the pros and cons of technology for society but to review some of the advances which have been achieved so far and to look at some developments likely to occur over the next few years.

The first technology we have to consider is one which is already widely used for the modification and change of human conduct and that is the use of drugs which have an effect upon the brain and nervous system to change the nature of the behaviour that the brain and nervous system produces. In one sense of course this is no new thing. Each society seems to have possessed its own substance for intoxicating and blotting out the mind, whether this be betel nuts, cocaine, alcohol, or marijuana. The widespread use of alcohol in our own society is a case in point where sanction has been given for the use of a drug known to radically change mental action and behaviour. It is known that alcohol consumed in relatively small quantities can destroy some of the millions of small cells of the brain, and that when consumed in large quantities over a protracted period of time have an even more severe effect. In acute states of alcoholism much of the fabric of the brain will have been destroyed and the person's mental life will be confused and disoriented.

We are also witness to another revolution instituted by the medical profession itself in the use of drugs to modify behaviour through the effect they have upon the brain and nervous system. For example, if we go to see our doctor we may well be given a tranquiliser, an antidepressant, or a stimulant. The consumption of tranquilisers reaches staggering proportions, nevertheless chemical therapy of emotional and psychological disturbance, in the control of highly overactive or aggressive behaviour, as well as in the alleviation of anxiety and associated symptoms could be seen as one of the triumphs of modern medicine. It is clear that a social revolution in our drug taking habits has taken place under medical aegis and that this pharmacological control over behaviour is something that has been quietly accepted because of the alleviation of suffering which it brings. Society, however, has still to consider and give its explicit consent to the revolution which has taken place in its midst with regard to how far the conduct and mental functioning of the individual may be changed as a result of pharmacological control.

Some of the most important advances of the next fifty to sixty years will be those where chemical substances are used to change the nature of the functions of the brain. The trend towards the development of drugs which have specific effects upon some aspects of human function but not others is something which may be expected to show further progress. Drugs to alter personality in one direction rather than another, drugs to enhance the range and capacity of human abilities and skills—as opposed to drugs which merely delude the person into thinking that his human capacities have been extended—drugs to increase drive, drugs to raise the level of intelligence and to speed the capacity for learning will be developed. We have passed through one pharmacological revolution and now we have to ask if we are about to pass through another.

We are now moving into the area where it is possible to use drugs to improve the level of intelligence and to speed the capacity for learning. There are a number of experiments carried out in animals where chemical substances can be employed to interfere with memory or to blot it out completely, in addition to experiments where the injection of some substances were found to increase the capacity of animals for learning and also to make the habits learned less resistant to change. The administration of ribonucleic acid or RNA is a case in point.

Patients suffering from senile conditions and organic pathology to the brain which has caused the power of their memory and intelligence to seriously deteriorate have also been found to improve after taking RNA and also another substance levodopa.

In 1964 Gordon and Helmer estimated in their report on a long-range forecasting study that in the year 2012 it would become feasible to use drugs to raise the level of intelligence (other than as dietary supplements and not in the case of just temporarily raising the level of apperception). We may not have reached the stage as yet where we can signify that the whole constellation of intellectual function in man can be raised by the use of drugs, but it is already apparent that we have moved a long way towards this possibility. We have been interested, in work which the author did with Pim Brouwers, in a drug called Piracetam® which has been shown over the course of experiments to improve learning in animals by its action on the brain. We carried out studies in which we gave this drug to volunteer human subjects and tested them on a variety of learning tasks. We gave our subjects lists of words to learn and found that those people who had been taking the drug slowly improved over the rest in their learning capacity and that after taking the drug for a fortnight their capacity for learning (words) had considerably increased. Although in this experiment we have not yet demonstrated an overall increase in the capacity for intelligent behaviour we have nevertheless done the next best thing and shown that Piracetam does improve the capacity for learning in the normal individual. If confirmed, some parts at least of what we call the capacity for intelligent behaviour can be improved by chemical means. In other terms, man's brain power can be increased by the use of drugs and apparently it is possible to work selectively to improve some parts of his mental makeup without necessarily acting at the same time to improve other parts.

The fact is that because this drug improves verbal learning it is a substance which is chemically capable of extending the intellectual functions of man. This drug does not delude the individual into feeling that he is doing well when in fact he is not, as do so many of the so-called psychoactive drugs. What it does is lead him on to achieve better things. We do not as yet know the bounds of its influence on mental action. We have demonstrated that it improves the intellect in one respect, but in principle our study shows that human brain power can be selectively increased by the use of drugs. The next step is to seek out other substances which also have an effect but upon other parts of the human mind. It may well be that the next drug revolution is at its beginning, where drugs are used not for kicks but for improvement in what the brain can achieve as measured by the yardstick of its performance.

The pharmacological revolution has proceeded apace in recent years. It is already apparent that ways of modifying human conduct and mental action have been found and that the action of doing this is now an integral part of ordinary medical practice. Yet although startling success has been achieved in the capacity to alter mood and to suppress and control agitated behaviour it is still the case that many of the most serious disorders which afflict the mind await their solution. Chemical therapy has taken enormous strides and we can cite as one of the great twentieth-century advances the medical care of the psychiatrically disturbed, but the technological revolution in the use of drugs for the treatment of mental illness is by no means complete.

A hopeful prediction is that if it is possible to use drugs to selectively act upon facets of mental life, to alter mood, to control agitated behaviour, and to increase learning capacity, then it may not be too long before substances are found capable of producing a radical alteration of the personality or otherwise capable of changing a person suffering severe psychosis into one more resembling the normal individual. To those who suggest that such an aim represents an attempt to make an unwarranted interference with the personal liberty of the individual, we can only point to the misery and suffering which psychosis brings about not only in its direct effect upon the person but also in the alienating and distancing effect of separating the sufferer from a natural relationship with the people around him.

Another feature of the technology of chemical use to affect the brain and nervous system has to be mentioned in this context. The technology in its aim is quite the opposite to that described previously. Good men and people who are kindly disposed can only feel abhorrence at the direction that this research has taken. As is well known, discussion has centred in recent years upon the possibilities of biological warfare and this has resulted in the development and indeed the manufacture of biological agents capable of destroying large numbers of the population. This is not all, for if newspaper reports are to be believed, development has also taken place to produce chemical substances which, when administered to the individual in the form of a gas or through other means, destroy an aggressor's or an opponent's will to resist and render him a relatively harmless and ineffective being. The impairment of the will to resist is a consequence of the action of the chemical agent upon the brain. The startling advances in the control of behaviour for therapeutic and clinical reasons does, as in other instances of technological advance, have its more sinister side and our description would not be complete if we failed to mention this or passed over this matter without drawing the reader's attention to it.

From the pharmacological revolution we turn now to another technological advance which although not having the same potential for wide-scale use nevertheless opens up exciting possibilities for treatment of the person on an individual basis. The techniques described in this context can best be grouped under the term biofeedback. One of the developments which concerns us is that where it is predicted that there will be a man-machine symbiosis and a feasibility of education by the direct implantation of information into the brain by electrical contact from outside sources. Although these are extrapolations relating more to science fiction than to fact, the foundation for this is at present being laid in those investigations where information is recorded electrically from the brain, and in which information is fed back into the brain by way of electrical stimulation through implanted electrodes, and in studies undertaken to establish direct electromechanical links into and out of the human brain.

The question of how far it is possible for an outside agent to control the functions of the mind is one which is frequently taken up in literature. It represents some of the deep-seated, archetypal fantasies and fears which social man may have about his future. In one sense this is precisely the function that we as individuals carry on in respect to the relationship between ourselves and others when we have conversation. We listen to what people say, we talk in return, and there is an instantaneous feedback, a communication of minds. This situation is obviously used and exploited to the degree to which one individual can influence others. Conversation is one of the great social therapies for good or ill—employed by friend, priest, social worker, politician, and doctor alike. Talking can be seen as biofeedback but this is not our explicit concern because we are interested in other avenues by which a technology of control can be established.

The question of feedback is one which has attracted considerable attention over the past few years not least for the practical possibilities of use which it opens up. Attempts have been made, for example, to gain access to the patient's emotional life and thought processes and to control these by the conditioning of socially relevant statements. The subjects are required to talk aloud about the experiences of their lives. A technician listening in an adjoining room increased the rate of clicking of a counter which determined the amount of pay to be given each time the subject began talking about significant emotional experiences. This was a technique used to get the subject to focus on the emotional part of his life and personality.

Other similar therapeutic arrangements have been devised. For example, employing simultaneous recording of electrical skin responses, if the patient talks about matters which personally "leaves him cold" a light remains off, but as soon as he discusses something with which he is closely and emotionally involved the light comes on and his task is to get the light on and keep it on as long as possible, meanwhile giving insight to the therapist on emotional matters of considerable significance.

It is perhaps the question of access to the electrical pathways into the brain which is most pertinent to our enquiries. In order to establish a linking up of the brain with machinery to establish a biofeedback situation, the conditions necessary are that it should be possible to get information from the brain and transmit information back into the brain. The problem is however a complex one even for clinical and therapeutic purposes and the technology is not easily achieved. We have discussed how Berger discovered the slow fluctuating wave which indicated something of the electrical functioning of the brain. We saw how, hand in hand with developments in electrical technology which allowed for greater amplification of a signal than had heretofore been possible, it became feasible to pick up the electrical message of the brain.

Access to the workings of the brain was gained and not only did many new insights stem from this source but the foundation stone was laid on which the new EEG technology was subsequently built. The existence of an electrical outflow channel from the brain enabled some of the functions of the brain to be measured in physical terms. However, in a sense, the measurement of the electrical activity represents a specialised and as yet poorly understood projection of the brain's activities. Another potent output channel is that which promotes the expression of behaviour—what the person says and what the person does. The activities of the brain are reflected in each minute movement, each twitch of the face and each of our most ordinary of verbal utterances.

The question of the physical control of the brain's electrical activity is the first step in control over the action of the brain by provision of feedback loops or through biofeedback. How far, for example, is it possible for the person to manipulate his own EEG activity by deliberate conscious activity? How far can subjects use their own brain waves to turn on lights of different colours? This was a problem studied by Barbara Brown. The three EEG frequency ranges of theta, alpha, and beta were used. When each was present in the subject's electrical record, they operated three lights of different colours. The subjects operated the lights by their own conscious effort so that they could control them and then identify what they thought the subjective mental states were (feeling and thoughts) which they found useful in bringing any one particular light into operation. The point about the results in this experiment was that by the use of the feedback loop many subjects were in fact able to control the nature of the electrical output of their own brains.

The second point is that this technique revealed that there were different subjective states associated with the different speeds of electrical activity of the brain. Alpha activity, for example, had pleasant feelings with increased awareness and tranquility, beta unpleasant thoughts and feelings in addition to excitement, whereas theta although difficult to categorise suggested the mental effort of problem solving or orienting.

Another extraordinary demonstration of the degree to which control can be effected over the electrical activity of the brain by conscious volition was that in which the EEG was used by the conscious person to communicate through to the outside world. When coupled to a fairly complex computer and a teletype it was found possible in another experiment for the subject using just his own EEG to type out morse code messages including the complete alphabet.

The time taken to transmit each character was slow, over half a minute on average, but as with muscle movements of the eyebrow, also used in typing out messages, the possibility exists of an output channel for those paralysed by stroke or other disorders. It has to be remembered also that the subjects were largely unpractised. It is after all a completely novel way of communication, and learning to write with your eyebrow or in whatever form is a slowly acquired art.

That a degree of control can be established over the electrical activity of the brain is demonstrated in these remarkable studies. However the question of control does not stop there. It is clear that a feedback loop into the brain, as well as one leading out, could play an important part in regulation of behaviour. Studies have been undertaken in this context of the effect of electrical stimulation through implanted electrodes. If, for example, the brain has been damaged and some of the functions are lost, we have to ask if the biofeedback network could allow some of these functions to be revived?

Damage to the motor system at one side of the brain renders the patient unable to use the limbs at the contralateral side. If it were possible to stimulate through implanted electrodes by remote control some of the lower centres for activation of the limbs, then it should also be possible to link up the electrode stimulation to patterns emanating from the patient's own brain and then, in principle, provide the individual once again with the capacity to exercise control over functions which had otherwise been lost. The difficulty lies in the fact not that a technology is not available which would make this possible but in our lack of knowledge of the functions of the human brain— the engineering aspect which permits the link to be created for the purpose of therapy.

The possibility of implanting circuits which use biofeedback techniques, where none exists in the brain or where pre-existing circuits have been destroyed, is an exciting one. When such techniques have been developed, the use of computers or even miniature logic circuits as a supplement to human function will be important.

However, it seems likely that there will be more simple applications of techniques of this kind before the more complex aspects can be put into practice. There are many interesting possibilities employing biofeedback loops. They could act as prosthetic devices upon which the person may rely just as he relies upon an artificial leg or upon a plastic heart valve. Is it possible to construct feedback arcs to span the gap where parts of the sensory system or parts of the nervous system have been destroyed or damaged?

Something of the principle of this can be seen in experiments on "seeing with the skin" in which the person who is blind is presented with pictorial input by virtue of the sensitivity of the skin and the fact that pictures of objects can be represented upon it. A panel of tactual stimulators placed upon the back of the individual can allow him to discern a picture of an object or to distinguish characters—letters of the alphabet or numbers useful in reading. A television camera is used to pick up the image, this is then transmitted to the skin on the subject's back by way of a matrix of mechanical stimulators. Success has been achieved and tests show that observers are able to perceive simple displays as soon as they are introduced to them.

They are able to perceive motion accurately and to imitate it with simple hand movements. If the subjects, both congenitally blind and blindfolded sighted subjects, were allowed to scan objects using the television camera themselves, they became quite successful at discriminating different forms. With practice, congenitally blind observers become proficient at identifying different objects and clearly skill can be acquired which gives the blind person an alternative means of observing the patterning of the world around him.

The limitation of systems of this sort at present relate largely to the poverty of the number of elements in the display, which in some of the original work was only 400. It is likely that greater sensitivity can be achieved with the provision of more detailed pictures as the number of tactual stimulator elements is increased.

Another development which attempts to bypass the deficiencies of a blind sense organ is to actually implant an array of stimulators directly into the visual areas of the human brain. Images picked up by television cameras could thus gain access to the brain and the blind individual would have some power of visual resolution restored through this means. So far the experiments conducted in this area show that some patterned vision from an array of this kind is possible and certainly experiences of light and dark appear but as yet the results provide no clear patterned vision.

In one of the first well known investigations, a fifty-two-year-old woman, totally blind after suffering bilateral glaucoma, received an array of eighty small receiving units implanted under the skin above the skull and terminating in platinum electrodes each leading in to the visual cortex which they contacted. This gave the subject of the experiment some very simple vision and elementary patterns of a very simple type could in fact be discriminated. It is possible that with a greater and greater array of stimulating agents much more effective vision could in fact be provided for the blind patient, although it must be said that the development of a truly effective device of this kind is still a long way away.

The question of a production of an artificial loop that will circumvent the ear in cases of deafness and gain access to the brain in spite of deficient sensory equipment is a problem of equal importance. The path along which the investigator must travel is a tortuous and difficult one and it is obvious that the future possibilities of useful communications by these means will be arrived at only slowly. There is no instant miracle. Nonetheless the indications are that such a device will ultimately be possible.

Electrodes have been implanted for experimental investigation in the auditory nerve of man bypassing the defective cochlea of the ear. The patient could perceive a variety of sounds and yet it was clear that what the patient could perceive through this means was limited. He could, for example, distinguish between different pulse rates up to 400 cps and some sensation was possible up to 1000 cps. He could discriminate reasonably well between different tunes, the tune sounding as though it were being played on a trumpet. The problem is, however, that the mature brain may not be able to completely unscramble messages given in this way, and it may be that the ear acts as a remote computer station to prepare the material for entry into the auditory part of the brain. Alternatively, the instrumentation for stimulating the auditory nerve may not be entirely satisfactory as a means of getting complex information into the nerve, or the brain itself may need time to learn how to deal with this uncharacteristic input. This research at any rate suggests the possibility that an artificial loop from a microphone into the auditory nerve could bypass a defective hearing organ and perhaps provide some rudimentary capacity for hearing.

Although dependent on highly sophisticated technological skills, these are not the most complete applications of biofeedback control that can be considered. The fact is that if an electrical current should be applied to the brain then a variety of behaviour patterns can be elicited. It is as though the current triggers a small section of the working machinery into activity just as the limbs of a puppet are moved and given animation when the appropriate string is pulled. It is therefore possible to exercise control not only of what enters into the brain but also, to some measure, what comes out.

Much of the work we discuss involves complex neurosurgery, the finding of an exact location in the brain and the implantation of electrodes in specifically chosen sites. It is therefore work of considerable complexity, but these types of investigation are in principle no more complex than many of the wonders of the present age and certainly a lot less complex than the design and building of a modern computer or the design of equipment for space flight.

The technical problems of this kind of biofeedback for research purposes can be simplified considerably in animal research by the use of those species which already employ electrical discharge as part of their inter-individual signalling systems or as part of their aggressive/defensive mechanisms. The electrical eel, for example, stuns and kills its prey by presenting it with an electrical discharge, by feeding that input into a computer something of the language of the electrical discharge can be understood and by the use of the computer appropriate electrical signals can be fed back to the fish. A relationship will ultimately be established in which the fish "talks" to the computer and the computer "talks" to the fish. It is possible for the human investigator not only to reach an understanding of the patterns of communication but also to exert a measure of control over the behaviour of the animal issuing commands to it.

In more advanced animals, behaviour can be controlled by the use of electrodes to stimulate the reward systems of the brain. As is well known there is an hypothalmic area towards the centre of the brain at the midbrain which when stimulated produces all the appearance of providing intense pleasure to the animal which will work to the point of exhaustion to receive more and more stimulation of this region. There are also complementary areas which seem to be associated with intense pain, the stimulation of which the animals will work strenuously to avoid. That these areas are bound up with the motive springs of behaviour seems to be a fact beyond doubt.

We have quoted the example of the pleasure areas of the brain to show that a technology could develop out of the brain studies, and that the chaining of patterns of brain stimulation with the ongoing activity of the brain can be used and has already been used as a means for promoting some activities on the part of the animal and diminishing others.

One word needs to be said about the technical aspect of this situation. The technological revolution in communication is a factor which has had its impact upon studies of the brain. Just as scientists had to await the development of the amplifier to record the electrical activity of the brain, so they waited for the development of telecommunication before it became possible to record the activity of the brain from a free moving subject or indeed to stimulate the brain in a free moving individual. Any idea of gaining access to the brain where the individual is permanently linked by a cable to the source of power supply is in danger of appearing absurd. In animal studies this has been possible because animals are confined to their cages and not allowed to move far. Wires acted as a chain binding the animal to the apparatus but modern developments make it possible to dispense with them. Telemetry, a wireless link between the animal and the stimulating source, is employed instead. The individual is free to move in any direction and without re-straint although at the same time it is possible for the investi-gator to stimulate or to record from the brain.

Telemetry techniques have been used for some years to study the physiological response of man, particularly in working or unusual environments. The technique mostly has been used to get information out. Heart rate, the electrical activity of the brain, and the workings of the autonomic system are easily transmitted. We must await sophistication in the use of this method for communication directly with the human brain by sending electrical pulses into the brain. The electrical message can be transmitted out but so also communication can be estab-lished inwards.

Yet if techniques exist for triggering parts of the brain into action at command, could it be that patterns of abnormal be-haviour and movement could be suppressed by techniques of this sort? Could the craving for drugs be suppressed by an electrode sited in the motivational systems of the brain; could undesirable aspects of behaviour and personality be changed?

Investigations have been undertaken over the course of many years to come to an understanding of those areas of the brain responsible for the initiation and control of aggressive behaviour. Aggression may be promoted by stimulation of the appropriate areas of the hypothalamus, so also may it be suppressed either by direct stimulation of other areas or through conditioning techniques which link the expression of aggressive behaviour in animals with a stimulating pulse to the pain centre of the brain. The human brain may not always be equated in structure and function with even man's closest relatives of the animal kingdom, nonetheless the centres for aggressive behaviour exist in the brain of man in much the same way as they do in cats, rats, or monkeys and the evidence for centres which promote aggressive behaviour in man is strong. What pertains in this instance to the brain of the animal also pertains to the brain of man.

It is possible to control aggressive impulses in man through the use of electrical stimulation to the brain; those people who are in fact unable to control their own violent disposition could, through surgery and electrode implantation, have such violence in their own makeup controlled for them. The application of techniques of this kind is feasible and realisable. The possibility of changing behaviour by gaining access directly to the brain is a formidable step but it is something which with the technological development of first the amplifier, second the telemetering system, and thirdly the computer is now already taking place and is an area in which we must expect major development in the future.

Studies have been undertaken which employ electrodes implanted directly into the brain of man for the purpose of recording the electrical activity taking place within when this is difficult to observe by conventional means. These investigations had the further purpose of locating a site within the brain from which aggressive outbursts originate with the object of destroying such areas either through surgery or through electrolytic lesion produced by the application of a current across the electrodes.

Delgado reports on electrodes implanted in the amygdala, that part of the brain concerned with aggressive behaviour; these implanted electrode recordings were of great value in determining if and where in this area of brain part should be destroyed to diminish the patient's highly aggressive behaviour. We quote a case report from Delgado.

This twenty-year-old white female had a history of encephalitis at the age of eighteen months. In addition she had experienced temporal lobe seizures and occasional grand mal seizures for ten years. She also had frequent rage attacks which on more than a dozen occasions resulted in an assault on another person. On one occasion she stabbed a complete stranger with a knife, on another she stabbed a nurse with a pair of scissors causing her serious injury. This patient would not be confined in the EEG recording room. Electrodes were implanted in the amygdala of her brain which through telemetry could be utilised at appropriate times. In fact, crises of assaultive behaviour reminiscent of her spontaneous bursts of anger could be elicited by radiostimulation of one of the controls placed in the amygdala. The patient on receiving this stimulus interrupted her ongoing activities, such as playing the guitar, and in a fit of rage threw herself against the wall, paced around the room for a few minutes, then gradually resumed her normal behaviour. This effect was repeated two days later with similar results. The fact that only one contact gave this type of response suggested that the surrounding neuronal field was involved in the behaviour problems of the patient. The use of stimuli fed into the brain proved to be critical in selecting the appropriate site of the brain to destroy for the elimination of these types of behaviour.

Animal experimentation has shown that it is possible to use telestimulation to inhibit behaviour in which one animal assaults or attacks another. It is also possible in animals to use electrical stimulation of the brain to increase or decrease appetites and to modify drives. The application of these findings for man is something which may well be as important as the use of electrical stimulation to modify the behaviour of aggression.

Use of the highly important neural systems of the hypothal-amus have been investigated in chronically ill patients who required neurosurgical treatment. Electrodes were placed in the reward systems in the brain of man. The patients responded by pressing a lever to gain brain stimulation but not necessarily more frequently than for more conventional forms of reinforce-ment. The patients were deteriorated and this investigation, although surprising by the fact that it was undertaken at all, showed little about the possible effectiveness of this work.

Another example of the use of implanted electrodes is for the relief from intractable pain. If the electrodes are implanted in the brain region responsible for the registration of pain then through their activation the passage of a current can be used to suppress the pain and relieve the individual of his suffering.

Other uses which may be suggested include those rare cases where damage to the brain stem in man leads him to assume a sleeping or an unconscious state of a permanent kind. So far physicians have been powerless to arouse the patient from this condition because the region responsible for the alertness of the brain has been destroyed or seriously interfered with. Our knowledge of the functions of this region of the brain and the development of a technology capable of stimulating the brain by remote control would now make it possible to use a system where an electrode implanted at the opposite side of the cut leading up into the pathways of the brain would, if stimulated, arouse the patient and lead him once more to enter the con-scious state.

Sleep and wakefulness would, of course, have to be under electrode control, but at least if successful a technique of this kind would allow such a patient to enter the waking state and to pass from a twilight world into one of conscious awareness.

The techniques of electrode implantation depend upon the process of complex neurosurgery. The possibility has to be entertained, bizarre though it may at first appear, that methods of access will be gained to the physical structure of the brain which do not depend upon opening the cranium or utilizing the complex paraphernalia of neurosurgical techniques. Much of what one might describe as the manipulative aspect of brain technology essentially awaits something of this kind. The possibility of stimulating the brain electrically without the actual implantation of electrodes into the brain has in fact already been studied. Observable effects could be produced on a patient when a current below the threshold which he could detect was passed from electrodes attached over the eyebrows to a neutral electrode placed on the leg. The psychological effects were observed when the current entered the brain by way of the orbital fissures.

There were a number of curious observations which stemmed from this work, each notable for the persistence and reliability with which the effect could be produced. In one female patient with involutional melancholia (a state of depression which comes about in old age) a regular fine tremor of both hands was produced during the flow of the current. This occurred each time the current was switched on. In another patient, a fifty-six-year-old male chronic schizophrenic who had been mute for about fourteen years, the onset of the current was associated with vocalisation and speech. After the onset of the current for a few minutes nothing happened, then verbalisation commenced and continued for an hour or so, although the current by that time had long ceased.

Perhaps the potentially most significant observation was the fact that mood changes appeared to be consistently and reliably associated with the onset and the nature of stimulation. When the scalp electrodes were positive (up to 500 mA) the subjects showed an upswing in their mood, there was an elevation of mood, there was an increase in alertness, and sometimes a tendency to giggle coupled with an increased involvement with the environment. If the scalp electrode produced a negative current flow, the patient showed a degree of withdrawal and quietness. In fact by observing the behaviour alone it was possible to judge with a fair degree of success the positive or negative direction of the current which had been administered to the subject. In this and subsequent investigations the results revealed that it is possible by gaining access to the brain, in this case without surgical intervention, and by the application of outside agents to produce changes of mood which in some cases lasted for periods appreciably longer than the application of the stimulus. In other words, a facet of the patient's personality had been altered by the effects of this technology applied to the brain. It need hardly be pointd out that there are many disorders of personality, depression as a case in point, where a change of mood is highly desirable. A variety of agents are employed in psychiatry to do this, some more effectively than others, but it is important to have an adequate understanding of the involvement of the brain in creating different moods, and even more so to tune those parts of the brain very finely towards different feeling states.

One of the closest parallels of the psychotechnology of the brain to everyday medicine is in the use of brain surgery to correct psychological ills. The fact of surgical intervention may be obvious in cases where the functions of the brain are slowly and progressively disturbed by invading pathology.

Physical conditions which affect the brain have a profound influence on behaviour and experience and the accumulated wisdom which makes a person what he is. Physical illness of the brain can affect the powers of judgement, the powers of reason and will, the intellectual abilities, the capacities for reason and insight, the ability to comprehend, the ability to remember and to deal coherently with the world. The personality of the individual may be radically changed by physical insult to the brain. Alcoholism is a case in point where there is deterioration of the brain which carries in its wake changes of the individual's abilities, personality, and life-style.

Physical damage to the brain often brings a disturbance of the fine balance and control which we regard as typical of normal functioning. If the brain is invaded by physical pathology then the disturbing effect which this has on the patient's mental functions is often only too evident. We have already argued that human abilities depend upon the integrity of the brain.

What about the question of the use of surgery to introduce a deliberate change into the patterning of the individual's behaviour? Is it justifiable, for example, that there should be neurosurgical treatment available to render the aggressive psychopath a relatively harmless individual—to ensure that such an individual takes a place in society? Many cases are reported of prefrontal leucotomy in which surgery was undertaken at the region of the frontal lobes of the cortex, usually for the relief of intense pain or anxiety which could not be controlled in other ways. The patient usually still continued to feel pain but was relieved of the care about it which made his life unbearable. The surgery although often successful was sometimes associated with undesirable personality changes usually attributed to disinhibiting effects. These took the form of uncontrolled behaviour, for example, losing judgement of the appropriateness of behaviour in social situations or becoming somewhat uninhibited. Some patients did in fact change from anxious and depressed individuals to socially disinhibited and uncontrolled personalities and this work was much criticised.

The question arises as to how far is it justified to interfere with the brain to promote more socially desirable aspects of the individual's personality?

When neurosurgery is undertaken to relieve conditions in which there is, for example, an invading pathology of the brain, the reasons for undertaking it are transparently obvious—this person will die unless he has this treatment. Where the question of the existence or not of life is no longer a relevant issue the question of whether there should be neurosurgical intervention becomes more debatable. Neurosurgery which has as its aim the transmutation of behaviour from one form to another is more problematical and the issue becomes highly controversial.

The major problem is the lack of knowledge which would make such transformations proceed with a high probability that they would succeed. Obviously the more successful the techniques of this kind are the greater the acceptance they would receive, at the present time success is a condition which cannot be guaranteed.

The problem is seen in its most acute form as it concerns the criminally insane. There are those people whose behaviour is so disturbed that they become a continuous burden to normal society. Such people require continuous vigilance. They are likely to harm others and institutionalisation is the only way in which society can, at present, cope with such individuals. Many such patients are violent offenders and many may be sexual criminals. Their insanity does not necessarily relate to the fact that they are exceptionally violent people but in some cases it does—in fact the insanity in such cases could be said to be the very incapacity from which they suffer.

If surgery were undertaken in such cases to render the person less violent and less prone to pursue a course of violent action then it is quite possible that such a person would be able to lead a more ordered life and one which it may be hoped could be acceptable to society at large. In the case of the person who is dangerously violent and uncontrolled, aggressive tendencies can, with increasing success and control, be ameliorated by surgery. The question must be asked, however, if techniques of this kind should be put into practice.

If the person is regarded as so dangerously violent as to be criminally insane then he may not be in a position to make a judgement on the facts that would lead to a rational agreement on the part of the patient to this form of treatment. There are considerable legal problems in addition to the technological, medical, ethical, and social problems. However, studies on the brain are proceeding apace, particularly as concerns the problems of aggression in animals and man, but it may well be that here, as in other instances, techniques exist but may well remain frozen because society is not prepared to give a mandate for their use.

The question of the treatment of sexual offenders is always a problematical one, particularly when the disorder is associated with criminal irresponsibility or indeed with insanity. The question of what remedy society should take to enable it to deal with a problem of this kind is equally open to debate. A variety of therapies are available for the treatment of the sexual offender, most are concerned with the question of causing a diminution of sexual drive. The person who is heavily sedated, for example, shows a greatly diminished sexual response. It is possible also to change sexual activity by the use of hormone administration, particularly in the case of the male offender, although side effects of this procedure may occur causing feminisation, development of breasts, and the loss of facial and body hair.

The possibility of a therapeutic approach to the brain is an alternative, albeit experimental, approach. Control over sexual behaviour is exercised by the brain. Implantation of hormones into the brain itself is capable of diminishing or heightening sexual activities in animals. There are circuits of the brain which respond directly to the amount of hormone circulating around them. The possibility exists of interfering with these circuits by the use of neurosurgical techniques to render them inoperative. Whether the abolition of such circuits could be conducted with the necessary selectivity remains to be seen.

The possibilities are there but what is clear from the examples so far cited is that the practical application of neuropsychology must go hand in hand with a deep and profound knowledge of the actions of the human brain. It is in the area of fundamental observation and information that we are still inadequately equipped. We do not as yet have the detailed knowledge of the circuitry of the brain which would enable an abnormality of function to be examined so as to allow the investigator to say that must be due to a fault in the functioning of circuit "xyz."

It is obvious that we need a practical understanding of the working circuitry of the brain. Only when this has been achieved will it be possible to fully implement the engineering approach which this work implies and to which it inevitably leads. We have witnessed great strides in our knowledge of the brain and in the application of this knowledge for the ultimate benefit of the patient and in particular for the relief of suffering. The work we have described is striking in its application, but how much more effective a neurosurgical approach to abnormal behaviour could be if we were in possession of a detailed knowledge and functional mapping of the brain.

There are many problems associated with the use of technological procedures and it would be foolish to deny or diminish the nature of these. In the first instance, there are the technical problems of actually putting such procedure into practice. Although theoretically it may be possible to conduct a series of manipulations upon the human brain, the actual act of doing them involves a highly complex and specialised realm of technology in itself. Also such techniques must rely for their application on accurate and fundamental knowledge of the working of the brain. Although our knowledge has increased greatly in recent years, to an extent which makes this kind of study possible at all, it is still the case that there are many areas of brain function where the application of techniques could fail simply because sufficient information about the workings of the brain is not at present available. In one sense it can be regarded as an important test of the power and validity of knowledge that it can seek a practical application.

With regard to the moral question, the use of psychotechnology as envisaged here may from one point of view be no different from the use of many medical or psychological procedures carried out for other reasons. If therapeutic benefits of a substantial kind result from the procedures then that in itself could be sufficient justification for their use. If a patient receives relief from intractable pain through the activation of an electrode implanted into the brain then that is all that is necessary for that procedure to be both therapeutically and morally valid.

There are considerations beyond this, however, where the therapeutic aim may be equally as valid but the moral question is a different one. How far is it justifiable to radically change personality as a procedure in its own right? How is it possible to say that the altered personality is one changed for the better, or indeed how is it possible to say that the change will be something more worthwhile and acceptable when there are so many different factors to be considered? The problem of the treatment of the criminal offender by the use of psychotechnological methods is also another area where moral and social considerations come to the fore.

The problem can be expressed in this way: How far is it justifiable to interfere with the brain of man to change his behaviour? There are those who argue that this is never justified even by the nature of the end results. They argue on the grounds of liberty and of the integrity of the individual and they suggest that any process that will radically change that person is something which no man should contemplate. Steven Rose has argued in his book *The Conscious Brain* that techniques such as those outlined may represent an inexcusable invasion of the individual's right to privacy. In the same way, there are those who would argue that attempts to cure the psychiatric patient are in reality a gross interference with that person's individuality and his freedom to adopt any life-style which he desires even though most people think it to be disturbed.

Yet common sense leads us to ask what is so special about these individual private realms? Are we not in danger of thinking of this as something more precious than in fact it is? (The middle-aged maiden may tremble at the moral lapses contemplated in her thoughts as she seeks absolution from her sins in the confessional but the priest has heard it all a thousand times before and the details of this lady's private life has little significance for him.) In evaluating the significance of psychotechnology the argument must not only be about questions of privacy but also about the equally moral question of whether the techniques permit pain and suffering to be relieved. It is in response to this question that the techniques which are used must ultimately seek their justification.

SUGGESTED READING LIST

Blakemore, C.: The Reith Lectures. Reprinted in *The Listener*, 1976.

Bogen, J. E.: The other side of the brain. I. Dysgraphia and dyscopia following cerebral commissurotomy. *Bull Los Angeles Neurol Soc, 34* (2):73-105, 1969.

Critchley, M.: *The Parietal Lobes*. London, Arnold, 1953.

Delgado, J. M. R.: *Physical Control of the Mind*. New York, Har-Row, 1966.

Dimond, S. J.: *The Double Brain*. London, Churchill, 1972.

Dimond, S. J.: The disconnection syndromes. In Williams, D.: *Modern Trends in Neurology*, Volume 6. London, Butterworths, 1975.

Dimond, S. J.: Brain circuits for consciousness. *Brain Behav Evol, 13:*376-395, 1976.

Dimond, S. J. and Beaumont, J. G. (Eds.): *Hemisphere Function in the Human Brain*. London, Paul Elek, 1974.

Eccles, J. C.: *Brain and Conscious Experience*. New York, Springer-Verlag, 1966.

Gazzaniga, M. S.: *The Bisected Brain*. New York, Appleton-Century-Crofts, 1970.

Geschwind, N.: Disconnection syndromes in animals and man. *Brain, 88* (II):237-294, 1965.

Heatherington, R. W.: *Current Problems in Neuropsychiatry*. Royal Medical Psychological Association, Ashford, Kent, Headly Bros, 1969.

Luria, A. R.: *The Man with a Shattered World*. London, Cape, 1973a.

Luria, A. R.: *The Working Brain*. Harmondsworth, Middlesex, Penguin, 1973b.

Maher, B. A.: *Principles of Psychopathology: An Experimental Approach*. New York, McGraw, 1966.

Magoun, H. W.: *The Waking Brain*. Springfield, Thomas, 1947.

McFie, J.: *Assessment of Organic Intellectual Impairment*. London, Academic Press, 1975.

Miller, E.: *Clinical Neuropsychology*. Harmondsworth, Middlesex, Penguin, 1972.

Newcombe, F.: *Missile Wounds of the Brain: A Study of Psychological Deficits*. Oxford, Oxford U Pr, 1969.

Penfield, W. and Roberts, L.: *Speech and Brain Mechanisms*. Princeton, New Jersey, Princeton U Pr, 1959.

Pribram, K. H.: *Languages of the Brain*. London, P-H, 1971.

Russell, W.; Ritchie, .; and Dewar, A. J.: *Explaining the Brain*. Oxford,

Oxford U Press, 1975.
Rose, S.: *The Conscious Brain*. London, Wiedenfeld & Nicholoson, 1973.
Schmitt, F. O. and Worden, F. G. (Eds.): *The Neurosciences Third Study Program*. Cambridge, Massachusetts, MIT Pr, 1973.
Schwitzgebel, R. L. and Schwitzgebel, R. K.: *Psychotechnology: Electronic Control of Mind and Behaviour*. New York, H R & W, 1973.
Williams, M.: *Brain Damage and the Mind*. Harmondsworth, Middlesex, Penguin, 1970.
Whitty, C. W. M. and Zangwill, O. L: *Amnesia*. London, Butterworths, 1966.
Zangwill, O. L.: *Cerebral Dominance and Its Relation to Psychological Function*. Edinburgh, Oliver and Boyd, 1960.

INDEX

223